DISCIPLINES OF A GODLY FAMILY

DISCIPLINES
of a
GODLY
FAMILY

KENT & BARBARA HUGHES

CROSSWAY BOOKS

A PUBLISHING MINISTRY OF
GOOD NEWS PUBLISHERS
WHEATON, ILLINOIS

Original edition copyright © 1995 by Kent and Barbara Hughes.

Revised edition copyright © 2004 by Kent and Barbara Hughes.

Trade paperback edition, 2007

Originally published 1995 by Tyndale House Publishers, Inc., Wheaton, Illinois with the title *Common Sense Parenting*

Published by Crossway Books
          a publishing ministry of Good News Publishers
          1300 Crescent Street
          Wheaton, Illinois 60187

Cover design: David LaPlaca

First printing, trade paper edition, 2007

Printed in the United States of America

ISBN 13: 978-1-58134-941-2

ISBN 10: 1-58134-941-6

Material from *Psalms of My Life,* copyright © 1987 by the estate of Joseph Bayly. Used by permission of Chariot FAMILY Publishing.

All Scripture quotations, unless otherwise indicated, are taken from *The Holy Bible, English Standard Version*, copyright © 2001 by Crossway Bibles, a publishing ministry of Good News Publishers. Used by permission. All rights reserved.

Scripture quotations marked RSV are taken from the *Revised Standard Version,* copyright © 1946, 1971 by the Division of Christian Education of the National Council of Churches of Christ in the United States of America and are used by permission.

Scripture quotations marked NIV are taken from *The Holy Bible: New International Version®*. Copyright © 1973, 1978, 1984 by International Bible Society. Used by permission of Zondervan Publishing House. All rights reserved. The "NIV" and "New International Version" trademarks are registered in the United States Patent and Trademark Office by International Bible Society. Use of either trademark requires the permission of International Bible Society.

Scripture quotations marked NASB are taken from the *New American Standard Bible,* copyright © 1960, 1962, 1963, 1968, 1971, 1972, 1973, 1975, and 1977 by The Lockman Foundation and are used by permission.

Scripture quotations marked NEB are taken from the *New English Bible,* copyright © 1970 by Oxford University Press and Cambridge University Press. Used by permission.

Library of Congress Cataloging-in-Publication Data
Hughes, R. Kent.
   Disciplines of a godly family / Kent and Barbara Hughes.—Rev. ed.
     p. cm.
   Includes bibliographical references and indexes.
   ISBN 1-58134-532-1 (alk. paper)
   1. Discipline—Religious aspects—Christianity. 2. Family— Religious
life. I. Hughes, Barbara. I. Title.
BV4647.D58H84   2004
248.4—dc22   2003021407

LB		17	16	15	14	13	12	11		10	09	08	07
15	14	13	12	11	10	9	8	7	6	5	4	3	2	1

To our mothers

LULA TRIGGS

and

BETH MULLER

*with love and deepest gratitude for their sacrifices
on our behalf*

A PSALM OF LOVE

Thank you for children
brought into being
because we loved.

God of love
keep us loving
so that they
may grow up whole
in love's overflow.

JOSEPH BAYLY

CONTENTS

PREFACE

Sometimes when we look through the family album and come to an early family photo, we become reflective. The photograph is a testament to the potential of every Christian family. Each child is an eternal soul who came into existence because of the love of his or her parents, something that could never happen to angels no matter how great their love. Each child is utterly original. Each has an eternal capacity for God. At the heart of every Christian family lies the hope that their children will come to know Christ early and will go on to full lives of service.

The beloved faces in our family album certainly do remind us that there is a lot of living ahead and, because the culture of a soul is a wild ride, some deep ups and downs. But we also recall that it is an elevating ride because the disciplined application of God's wisdom to the family has, over the years, raised the spiritual capacities of both parents and children.

Disciplines of a Godly Family is, above all, a celebration of a biblically informed view of parenting and of the family. What we offer here is wisdom culled from forty years of marriage and childrearing. Our advice is consciously practical. It is not comprehensive because it comes from the unique circle of our lives. But what we will relate will find resonance in the hearts of those who are attempting to parent under the authority of God's Word.

We were not perfect parents with model children, though today they are all exemplary Christians. Rather, ours is an eloquent witness that imperfect people, from less than perfect backgrounds, can by God's grace raise a joyous Christian family.

What we share is personal, an intimate album of childrearing. It is our family's gift to you.

Introduction: Thinking
Christianly About the Family

L ife wasn't easy for us in the summer of 1963. Here is how Barbara recalls that summer:

> Kent was both a full-time college student and a full-time swing-shift worker in a factory in East Los Angeles. I was two weeks away from the delivery of our first child.
>
> Though we had saved carefully and lived on very little, school was so expensive that, according to our calculations, we would only have about $160 when the baby arrived — not nearly enough for the anticipated hospital cost of $250 and the doctor's fee of $250. We had no idea what to do — except pray.
>
> What happened is unforgettable. I went to the doctor for my regular checkup. As the doctor, who was not a churchgoing man, perused my chart, he noticed that Kent was planning to attend seminary. He asked a couple of questions, then casually remarked, "We don't charge the cloth." I was perplexed: "What's the cloth?" He explained that cloth meant the clergy — preachers. All that we now needed was the $250 for the hospital.
>
> When the night came for the birth of our lovely daughter Holly, Kent put on his Sunday best and escorted me to the hospital for the sacred event. Perhaps the doctor was just being kind when he said that Kent was the most excited father he had ever seen. We like to think it was true.

There was only one problem: Kent had only $163 in his wallet. When he returned to claim his two "girls" and stood nervously before the cashier, waiting for the bill, he tried to think of what to say to convince her that he would pay. She then presented him with the grand total: $160. She explained that I had been admitted just as the day was changing, so we were charged for one less day.

With the extra three dollars in hand, Kent ran from the cashier to the florist with just enough money to lavish a bouquet on his wife.

These events surrounding the birth of our first child are not only a landmark in our family history — they also foreshadow the main themes of this book. Here are those themes:

• The family is the object of God's special concern. Perhaps we can even say that God is on the side of the family against the vicissitudes of life.

• Realistically speaking, in a fallen world the family is always in a precarious state (financially and in other ways).

• A Christian family is dependent on God's grace and providential care to see it through the difficulties that are an inevitable part of family life. No family is strong enough to manage its affairs apart from God's provision.

• In view of these things, parents should embrace the ups and downs of family life as comprising one of the chief arenas in which they relate to God and to each other.

• Parents should consciously organize the history of their family into a story of divine providence; they should not let the events of family history simply be lost or forgotten.

• God can be trusted to bless the families of believers. This is not to deny that terrible tragedies engulf some families; it is only to say that it is in the nature of God to provide for and bless his people.

August 10, 1963, became a treasured stone of remembrance for the two of us. God miraculously met our needs, giving us a substantive sign of his smile upon our family. And the undiminished joy of that occasion was repeated three more times in the next few years — each time with increased intensity of joy. As a matter of fact, the birth of our first child set the tone for the entire experience of raising our family of four to maturity. It has been a continuing celebration.

All of our children were born before Kent finished seminary; so those early years were lean. Although the doctor who delivered Holly did not charge "the cloth," other service providers and retailers did! But through the succession of clunker cars, the "doing without" while others had money for things, we were joyous . . . and the joy persisted. Today, past midlife, after more than forty years of marriage and eighteen grandchildren, we can say that our family, with its natural ups and downs, is an unceasing source of joy. We only have one regret — that we didn't have more children.

Of course, not everyone feels as we do about parenting. The visible public lives of our time, from Winston Churchill to Gloria Steinem, chronicle the tragedy of those who had a parent or parents who for one reason or another neglected their role. It is no surprise that Churchill's diseased, self-absorbed father was so neglectful of his pathetically needy son, or that Gloria Steinem's revulsion for motherhood was related to her pathetically needy mother. Such neglect is now commonplace in the world.

What is surprising, however, is that a similar malaise is often found among professing Christians. We have personally counseled men and women whose churchgoing, Bible-reading parents have frankly told their children that they wished they had never given birth to them. Still more have confided that, while their parents were never so direct, they nevertheless conveyed that their children had thwarted their potential. One young man told us that he could not remember a day when his missionary mother did not remind him that she had sacrificed her ministry potential to have a family. She actually believed that the children were holding her back. But more often the telltale sign among Christian parents of a defective parental perspective is an ambivalence about family. Outwardly these parents give lip service to the privilege of parenting, but inwardly they carry the attitude that parenting is a burden to be endured.

BEHIND THE CONFUSION

How do such attitudes come to dwell in Christian hearts? First, many people are captive to a culture that defines self-worth and fulfillment in terms of contribution, name, education, and money. Society applauds the person who designs a building more than it does the one who attends to the architecture of a child's soul. Our culture values a face that is known to the public far more than it does a countenance reflected in a child's eyes. The world sets a higher priority on attaining a degree than on educating a life. It values the ability to give things more than it does giving oneself. This approach to self-worth has been relentlessly sown by modern culture and has taken root in many Christian hearts, so that there is no room for another self — even if it is one's own child.

Another factor that regularly contributes to the parenting-is-a-burden attitude is the inconvenience of pregnancy and early childrearing. Eric and Julie had been married for three carefree years when Julie became pregnant. Both proudly welcomed the pregnancy and happily announced it, to the congratulations of family, friends, and church. Soon, however, Julie's initial enthusiasm was dampened by morning sickness, which for her became a perpetual *mal de mer* — seasickness — with no port in sight. Gradually Julie's nausea lifted, and she began to eat — and grow and grow. She was pregnant and fat, and she felt ugly — despite Eric's remonstrances. Neither was very happy. Their sex life had taken a nosedive when she was so sick, and now, understandably, it wasn't at its optimum.

Eric was secretly resentful, and Julie was bored and vaguely fearful. She missed her friends at work and wondered how well she would perform at delivery. "That little person in there," they mused, "has sure changed things."

Caleb's birth went reasonably well, but he was colicky and susceptible to ear infections. Julie and Eric were in for several months of interrupted sleep and messy tasks that they both resented. Of course, they both loved Caleb intensely. That never changed.

But Julie did not sense that she was a good mother and began to feel inadequate. So she did the natural thing — she minimized and even avoided that which made her feel inadequate. Her unhappiness made dieting difficult, so the weight stayed on. One morning as Julie was cuddling Caleb, she teasingly said, "You cost me — I lost my figure over you." It was a refrain baby Caleb was to hear again and again. Meanwhile, Eric found himself a little jealous of Caleb. Caleb was getting the attention *he* once had received from Julie.

The prevailing attitudes toward family coupled with the necessary inconvenience of pregnancy and childrearing have poisoned the perspective of many young couples, though they are sons and daughters of the church. Not only are there scores of parents who consider family to be inhibiting, but there is also a growing number of young couples who are putting off a family until they have achieved professional success and thus will be able to minimize the inconvenience through their wealth or by limiting their family to one or two children.

What is needed is a renewed understanding of the foundational principles of the Christian family — principles on which the disciplines of a godly family can be built. Without a firm foundation, the disciplines are unlikely to flourish. The right foundation is rooted in God's Word.

WHAT THE BIBLE SAYS ABOUT THE FAMILY

When our first child came, we announced her birth with a joyous line from the psalmist's praise of children: "Children are a heritage from the LORD" (127:3). This declaration is a concise expression of the age-old regard that God's covenant people had for children. Indeed, the opening chapter of Holy Scripture records the divine commission to "be fruitful and multiply" (Gen. 1:28), and later chapters of Genesis record the anxiety of the barren and the praise of those who give birth. Israel's aged princess, Sarah, and her husband, Abraham, named their firstborn Isaac, which means "laughter," for great was their joy at God's gift.

Not only do the Scriptures celebrate children, but they laud as blessed those who have been given many. Psalm 127:3-5 exults,

> *Behold, children are a heritage from the LORD,*
> *the fruit of the womb a reward.*
> *Like arrows in the hand of a warrior*
> *are the children of one's youth.*
> *Blessed is the man*
> *who fills his quiver with them.*

The Purpose of a Family: Glorifying God

Scripture's declaration that children are a blessing emphasizes their significance to God's people here on earth and summarizes what the Christian's attitude ought to be regarding parenting. But children also have a vertical significance, which is often passed over in today's discussion of family — namely, the glory of God.

The Westminster divines, after a long and measured look at Scripture, unanimously declared that "the chief end of man is to glorify God and to enjoy him forever." This principle governs every human relationship, but it begins in the sacred structure of the family, where people are most profoundly shaped. God is glorified, of course, when his children's lives radiate his character — which only the Son could perfectly do, for "he is the radiance of the glory of God and the exact imprint of his nature" (Heb. 1:3). Because Christ perfectly represented God, our children, if they truly come to God in faith, can by grace radiate more and more of his character. It is our joyous heavenly commission to lead them to Christ and then influence their life so they walk increasingly in the way of grace.

This is our great business, as Robert Dabney wrote long ago:

> The education of children for God is the most important business done on earth. It is the one business for which the earth exists. To it all politics, all war, all literature, all money making ought to be subordinated; and every parent especially ought to feel, every hour of the day, that next to making his own calling and election sure, this is the end for which he is kept alive by God — this is his task on earth.[1]

How elevating it is to realize that your family is the divinely ordained and primary vehicle to bring glory to God.

How to REALLY Influence Society

In this respect, parenting — not politics, not the classroom, not the laboratory, not even the pulpit — is the place of greatest influence. To suppose otherwise is to be captive to the shriveled secular delusion. We must understand that it is through the godly family that God's grace, a vision of God, a burden for the world, and a Christian character are most powerfully communicated.

In the Old Testament, when God chose to lead his people, the Bible repeatedly indicates that he looked for a person (see Isa. 50:2, 10; 59:16; 63:5; Jer. 5:1; Ezek. 22:30). A single holy individual can make all the difference in this world. We must not succumb to the deceptive mathematics of worldly thinking that considers the pouring out of one's life on a hidden few as a scandalous waste of one's potential.

Parents, don't abandon your place of influence. It is still true that "the hand that rocks the cradle rules the world." Believe it.

Sanctification

Paul wrote in 1 Thessalonians 4:3 that "this is the will of God, your sanctification." Parenting is profoundly sanctifying. When we were first married, the new relationship revealed rooms of selfishness in our lives — and within those rooms doors to other rooms, and in those rooms yet other doors and closets. The revelation was the beginning of an ongoing, lifelong housecleaning. And the addition of children truly deepened the process. The inconvenience of parenting — the self-giving, the prayer, the dependence upon God, the growth — can be an experience of sanctification like no other.

C. S. Lewis put it this way when he explained family love: "Dogs and cats should be brought up together. . . . It broadens their minds so."[2] The discipline of parenting can be the road to an enlarged soul and the path to unimagined heights of spiritual development. That's the way God planned it.

The Satisfactions of a Christian Family

Here we can categorically say that no professional accomplishment, no honor, no "success" comes close to the satisfaction of family. Of course, our grown children are not perfect. After all, they had us for parents! Nor do we always see eye-to-eye on everything. But our children's sails are set to go with Christ, to buck the winds of culture, to follow wherever he leads — and they are good sailors. Satisfaction? Definitely.

We are optimistic about our family because it continues to be an increasing source of *blessing, glory, power, sanctification,* and *satisfaction.*

DISCIPLINING YOUR ATTITUDE

If you've fallen prey to worldly attitudes about children, how can you regain a sense of godly joy in the little people whom God has given you to raise? The following steps may help you come to a biblical perspective:

1. *Personalization.* Write in the appropriate names to complete this statement:

_____[your child/children] is/are a heritage from the Lord. The fruit of _____'s womb is a reward. Like arrows in the hand of a warrior are _____ [your children], the children of _____'s youth. How blessed is _____ [father's name], who fills his quiver with them (Ps. 127:3-5).

2. *Resolution.* I resolve to keep before me the larger picture — the chief end of my task — the glory of God. I will consciously devote my prayers, my ambition, my domestic energies to God's glory.

_____

Name and Date

3. *Repentance and prayer:* Dear Father, I confess to you that today my heart has been captive to wrong thinking that says what I am doing as a parent is unimportant, a waste of my gifts. I repent of this and ask you to help me think your thoughts regarding the value of my task in caring and providing for this child [these children]. In Jesus' name, Amen.

OR

Lord, I've allowed the discomforts and inconveniences of parenting to sour my attitude and rob me of the pleasure of cherishing my children as I ought. Please deliver me and fill me with satisfaction and joy. In Jesus' name, Amen.

4. *Thankfulness.* Thank God for your children, and ask him to teach you how to use your divinely given power to grace the life of each of your offspring, so that when God looks for a man or woman, he or she will be found.

Over the years Kent has held hundreds of babies as their parents present them to God before the church family. As he takes children in his arms, he sometimes comments on their exquisite little hands so wondrously hinged; their amazing inner complexity — a rainbow tapestry of veins and nerves; their racing, tiny, valved heart. He speaks of how each body, fresh from God's mint, hints metaphorically at the subtlety of the person, brimming with intelligence, and at each one's soul, as unique as the child's fingerprints, with an equally unique capacity for God.

We pray for their parents. We pray that they may glimpse the glory and privilege of parenthood — for their attitude is going to make all the difference.

BUILDING
A
FAMILY

1

Discipline of Establishing a Heritage

A vital element for building a family is instilling a healthy sense of heritage — an appreciation of family roots, both earthly and spiritual. Yet it is increasingly common in our world for children to have no such sense of continuity or regard for family history. Too many feel that they have come from nothing and are bound for nothing — and this goes for Christians, too. Family heritage is a subject of neglect that is in need of rehabilitation. It is one of the disciplines of a godly family.

Psalm 127:4 compares children to arrows. Parents, like archers, launch their children into the future, aiming toward a distant target. Some parents take clear aim, and their arrows are well directed toward their future mark. But other "child arrows" are fired from undisciplined bows by parents who are, at best, ambivalent about where they came from and unsure of their aim. Their arrows waver and falter, then finally succumb to gravity with no mark in sight. They tragically prove the adage, "If you aim at nothing, you'll surely hit it."

One essential element in giving direction to one's children is *heritage*. Understanding where we came from, and even more, having some appreciation for it, will help us supply healthy direction.

All our heritages are flawed, of course, some far more than others. Modern men and women are so sensitized to this that many have come to use the sins of their parents as a cloak for their own sins and parental deficiencies. As Robert Hughes wrote in *Time* magazine, this has brought "the rise of cult therapies teaching that we are all the victims of our parents, that whatever our folly, venality, or outright thuggishness, we are not to be blamed for it, since we come from 'dysfunctional families.'"[1]

Tragically, we have known second- and third-generation Christians who have bought into this misguided and erroneous logic. They nurse deep bitterness because, for example, their parents were rigid legalists or hypocrites. These hurts become convenient excuses for the skewed trajectories of their own lives. And then, because they themselves are so far off course, they further misdirect their own precious arrows, producing children who falter without stability and direction.

The reality is that all of us, of every generation, live in families that are dysfunctional in varying degrees. We all make mistakes; we sin against our children, and they against us. Life is often (perhaps for most) unfair and even cruel. Although we are not to blame for others' actions against us, we must assume responsibility for our own actions and failings. To focus on injustice is to provide a grim, corrosive heritage for the next generation.

THE DISCIPLINE OF BUILDING A POSITIVE HERITAGE FOR YOUR FAMILY

Families can prove highly skilled at nursing a bitterness regarding some wrong suffered. Consider the fictional case of the Doe family. Early on, each new child in the family discovers that your father's Uncle Ted can't be mentioned without evoking a negative response: "He was the stingiest miser in Iowa." In reality, back in the 1960s he refused to give a loan to his brother (your grandfather). But he also has a great sense of humor, takes his nephews fishing, and gives all the children their first piggy bank. Nevertheless, the bitter epithet is beyond erasure. Uncle Ted is condemned to be a "tightwad" in the family's eyes no matter what he does.

The Discipline of Forgiveness

The discipline of forgiveness is essential to building your family and enhancing your heritage. As a girl, Barbara learned some important lessons about forgiveness through difficult experiences with her father. She recalls:

I was just fourteen years old that warm June day as I readied myself for graduation from Stephens Junior High School. I was about to receive the Daughters of the American Revolution Award for citizenship, scholarship, and service to one's school, and I was to address the graduates. Nervously, I scanned my notes and straightened the hem of my new blue organdy dress, which Grandma Barnes had lovingly made for me.

As I began to ascend the platform, one of my girlfriends ran to me giggling, "There's a drunk man over there!" Dad's noisy arrival was unavoidably conspicuous. His clothes were a mess, and he was so intoxicated that he had difficulty staying on his feet as he walked to his place. Dad's struggle with alcohol had always been a source of fear and pain in our family, but now it was the cause of my personal public humiliation.

I began to pray. And that prayer helped me to get through the painful situation. My trembling legs nearly gave way as I rose to speak, but inside something solid and good was taking place. I wasn't experienced enough to fully comprehend it. But I did understand that my father, my daddy, was causing me pain and that my heavenly Father had taught me to forgive: "And forgive us our debts, as we also have forgiven our debtors" (Matt. 6:12). So as the principal presented the award, tarnished now of its anticipated glory, I made a decision. *By the grace of God* I would not hate my father. I would *forgive* him. Then I began my speech.

At the ceremony's end, while we were congratulating one another and saying our summer good-byes, I took my father by the hand and introduced him to my favorite teachers.

There was no way Barbara could know how momentous her decision was, but her life would have taken a far different course had she become embittered. God's grace was adequate to help her, and because of his forgiving mercy, her heritage did not sour. As Christians, we must discipline ourselves by God's grace to forgive and forget the wrongs done to us.

The Discipline of Being Positive

Forgiveness is closely related to the discipline of cultivating positive attitudes. In the years that followed Barbara's graduation, her father's drinking weighed terribly on the family. Her father finally landed on skid row in Los Angeles, where he remained until he was diagnosed with advanced emphysema. He returned home as an invalid, and his wife cared for him for eleven years before his death.

That decade provided our children's memories of their grandfather. During that time we determined to emphasize the positive about Grandpa. We talked about his great sense of humor (he was outrageously funny), what terrific chili he made, and how good he had been at fishing for shark off Rainbow Pier. We laughed when he tried to yodel, croon, or play chords on the old piano. We entranced our own children (and Grandpa!) when we scooped them up and danced the two-step that he had taught us years earlier. Today we all extravagantly make a fuss over babies — any babies — partly because Grandpa did. He was so utterly captivated and charmed by the sweetness of infants that whenever he held one, he was a delight to behold. And he passed that on to us. He also loved to garden — something that has become Barbara's passion.

This is but a small part of his legacy to our family. Our children never learned about that painful graduation day when Barbara was fourteen until they were grown and Grandpa was long since in heaven. We experienced the benefits that come from the discipline of being positive about our family heritage.

The Discipline of Focusing on the Good

As a boy, Kent suffered a major deficiency in his upbringing. His father, Graham Hughes, was killed in an industrial accident when Kent was four years old. Kent's memory of his father is a flickering, candlelit vision of a slender man with red, wavy hair, "asleep" on the champagne satin of his casket. Kent was bereft of a male role model and destined to be raised with his little brother by his widowed mother, widowed grandmother, and widowed aunt. He had no male to teach him manly things.

Being raised in an all-female household could have been a great disadvantage, except for this: Kent's mother consciously made up for it by taking her boys camping every summer at Big Sur, teaching them to fish with Grandpa Bray's fly rods, and presenting them with Grandpa's guns at the proper age. Young fathers also took an interest in Kent. Eddie across the street showed him how to dress game, and Jim, who lived with his young wife in the apartment behind Kent's family, taught him to build model planes. And of course Christian men of his church took special interest in him during his teenage years: his pastor, Verl Lindley; his youth sponsor, Howard Busse; and Robert Seelye, who shepherded him in his college years. Divinely tailored benefits issued from a terrible loss. Kent has a unique, enviable, godly heritage, allowing him to echo what David said in Psalm 68:5-6: "Father of the fatherless and protector of widows is God in his holy habitation. God settles the solitary in a home."

The Discipline of Beginning Something New

Obviously, when the two of us came together and began a family, we did not come perfectly equipped for the job. One of us had no father, and the other had what today would be termed a dysfunctional father. We had to start where we were with what we had. But what we had was substantial. We had the powerful, quiet examples provided by our mothers, who had daily laid down their lives for us, and we had the promises that God makes to those who follow him. We were beginning a great adventure, and the last thing on our mind was self-pity or remorse over what we didn't have. There was fresh land before us to clear and settle, and we brimmed with hope.

Today we minister in a church that is 130 years old, rich with heritage and tradition. But thirty years ago we pioneered a brand-new church. Absolutely everything we did that first year was "original." We were privileged to decide which traditions the church would be practicing for many years into the future. We saw that as an opportunity to make an impact on the church for generations to come. And that's exactly how we viewed our family. We got to start something new. Our deficiency was the ground of our opportunity.

Like dry sponges, we soaked up every bit of wisdom we could gain from experienced Christian families. There was much trial and error. Nearly everything we did was done imperfectly. It wasn't our adequacy that God used to accomplish his purposes in our family, nor will it be yours. Rather, God's work begins for everyone, regardless of circumstances, with an attitude of disciplined dependence on him for what is necessary to live the Christian life. The accompanying virtues of such dependence are faith, prayer, and obedience — faith that God will accomplish what he has promised, a life of dependent prayer, and a determined obedience to do God's will.

BUILDING ON YOUR ETERNAL HERITAGE

In building a heritage, Christians have a vast advantage over those who do not know Christ. Scripture says, "If anyone is in Christ, he is a new creation. The old has passed away; behold, the new has come" (2 Cor. 5:17). Gone with the old are a life dominated by sin and the power of destructive relational habits that inhibit a healthy heritage; come are a new heart, the indwelling of the Holy Spirit, and a new moral sensitivity and power to do right. No matter what your past heritage, all is new in Christ. Christians have a deep reservoir of heritage from which to draw — one that is grounded not in fleeting life but in eternity.

Paternal Heritage

At the heart of our heritage is the paternity of God, who is our devoted, loving Father. A telltale sign of our relationship with God is the powerful inner impulse to address him as our dearest Father: "You have received the Spirit of adoption as sons, by whom we cry, 'Abba! Father!'" (Rom. 8:15); "And because you are sons, God has sent the Spirit of his Son into our hearts, crying, 'Abba! Father!'" (Gal. 4:6). This awareness of God's paternity is meant to instill a sense of continuity and security in us as cherished members of God's household. J. I. Packer has written:

> If you want to judge how well a person understands Christianity, find out how much he makes of the thought of being God's child, and having God as his father. If this is not the thought that prompts and controls his worship and prayers and his whole outlook on life, it means that he does not understand Christianity very well at all. For everything that Christ taught, everything that makes the New Testament new and better than the Old, everything that is distinctively Christian, is summed up in the knowledge of the Fatherhood of God the Father.[2]

Relating to God as Father can be difficult for those who have had extremely poor earthly fathers, but it is not impossible because everyone can *imagine* what a good father is like. As parents we must discipline this blessed reality into our minds as essential to our heritage — right now, in this world. We must passionately believe it.

Family Heritage

With a disciplined focus on God as Father, we will experience an increased sense of heritage in the church, which is God's eternal family. Our mutual paternity, our shared impulse to cry, "Dear Father," enhances our sense of belonging. To call God "Father" means that in the body of Christ we have spiritual brothers, sisters, fathers, mothers, and children (see Mark 10:29-30) — a sublime heritage that is closer than blood relationships and will grow yet sweeter and sweeter.

In praying for his Ephesian family, Paul prayed that "having the eyes of your hearts enlightened . . . you may know . . . the riches of his glorious inheritance in the saints" (Eph. 1:18). Paul wants us to see that *we are God's riches* — his glorious inheritance, his heritage. Christ's heritage is our heritage, and our heritage is Christ's. If this does not make our hearts sing, what will?

DISCIPLINES THAT WILL HELP YOU GET STARTED

Whatever you and your spouse's backgrounds — even if you have no spouse and feel hopelessly alone — you can build an enduring sense of heritage that will extend to your children and their children. Here are some disciplines to help you get started:

1. *List the deficiencies and injustices of the past, then choose to work toward forgiving them.* The following Scriptures will be helpful in forgiving others:

> *Put on then, as God's chosen ones, holy and beloved, compassion, kindness, humility, meekness, and patience, bearing with one another and, if one has a complaint against another, forgiving each other; as the Lord has forgiven you, so you also must forgive.*—Col. 3:12-13

> *Forgetting what lies behind and straining forward to what lies ahead, I press on toward the goal for the prize of the upward call of God in Christ Jesus.*—Phil. 3:13-14

2. *When you have made this choice, don't attempt to accomplish it in your own strength.* Draw on the grace of Christ every single day, lifted up by Bible passages such as these:

> *I can do all things through him who strengthens me.*—Phil. 4:13

But he said to me, "My grace is sufficient for you, for my power is made perfect in weakness." Therefore I will boast all the more gladly of my weaknesses, so that the power of Christ may rest upon me.—2 Cor. 12:9

He who calls you is faithful; he will surely do it.—1 Thess. 5:24

3. *List the good things you received from your parents.* Even if your situation was almost totally destructive, you still received the color of your eyes and hair, your physique, your innate abilities, and life itself. Now thank God for those gifts, with verses such as these filling your consciousness:

Give thanks in all circumstances; for this is the will of God in Christ Jesus for you.—1 Thess. 5:18

Giving thanks always and for everything to God the Father in the name of our Lord Jesus Christ.—Eph. 5:20

With thanksgiving let your requests be made known to God. And the peace of God, which surpasses all understanding, will guard your hearts and your minds in Christ Jesus.—Phil. 4:6-7

4. *Now make a wish list of all of the things you would like to pass on as a legacy to your children and grandchildren* — attitudes, spiritual inheritance, interests, etc.

As Christians, we all stand on level ground before the cross. We are all new creatures with a God-given sense of *paternity* and *family*.

FOOD FOR THOUGHT

Are all families dysfunctional? Why? To the same degree?

What does the phrase family heritage suggest to you? If you were asked what your family's heritage is right now, what would you say? What do you want it to be?

What does Barbara's story convey to you about forgiveness?

Why do Christians have an advantage over others when it comes to building a heritage?

What do Romans 8:15 and Galatians 4:6 reveal about the heart of your heritage? What does the title for God there mean to you personally?

2

Discipline of Promoting Family Affection

W e invited our relatives and friends to witness the joyous occasion, and we armed them with streamers and confetti. As our son Kent walked across the platform to receive his high school diploma, we thundered in unison, "Way to go, Kent!" and showered the sedate audience with the confetti and streamers. They loved it! And Kent? He flashed a big smile because he knew it was his day of victory — and our excuse to proclaim our affection.

Disciplines for Nurturing Family Affection

Family affection is not the same as family love. Most people have the common-sense knowledge that says we are supposed to love our family members. In fact, it is generally understood that no matter what difficulties they may present, we stand by them — simply because they're "family." This kind of love springs from a sense of loyalty and duty.

Family affection, on the other hand, involves genuinely *liking* each other. Here you actually enjoy being together. Phyllis McGinley says it well:

> Happy families . . . own a surface similarity of good cheer. For one thing, they like each other, which is quite a different thing from loving. For another, they have, almost always, one entirely

personal treasure — a sort of purseful of domestic humor which
they have accumulated against rainy days. This humor is not necessarily witty. The jokes may be incomprehensible to outsiders,
and the laughter spring from the most trivial of sources. But the
jokes and the laughter belong entirely to the family.[1]

That is why everyone in our family chuckles when we see a bull-
dozer. We are reminded how, as a preschooler, Carey inadvertently called
them "dullbozers," and the name stuck. We all still prefer it.

We have found that affection flourishes through three disciplines:
loving God, loving each other, and communicating.

Loving God

Looking back to the early days and years of our marriage, we realize that
we began with the best possible foundation for building affection: love
for God. Though we brought little to our marriage in the way of finan-
cial resources or relational experience, we were rich in our commitment
to love and obey God.

Love for God is foundational because it puts us in touch with the
source of love (1 John 4:8) and gives us an *example* of ideal love (1 John
4:10-11). But most importantly, it *empowers* us to love in the manner that
duty demands. "We love because he first loved us" (1 John 4:19). We are
able to love God and others through the reception of God's love. Loving
God is what makes other loves endure. This discipline, the day-by-day
empowerment to live out this love for people who aren't always "lov-
able," is what fosters the ongoing growth of affection.

Loving Each Other

Husbands and wives are supposed to love each other. The Scriptures
leave no doubt, and children instinctively know that this is true (Eph. 5
— 6). It is essential, then, if a family is to develop the bonds of affection,
that the children have the assurance of their parents' love for one another.
Elton Trueblood puts it like this:

> It is the father's responsibility to *make* the child know that he is
> deeply in love with the child's mother. There is no good reason
> why all evidence of affection should be hidden or carried on in

secret. A child who grows up with the realization that his parents are lovers has a wonderful basis of stability.[2]

True love between parents cannot help but show. Children will hear love in the tender words exchanged when parting or even in the restrained tone of voice that is used when someone is angry. They will see love in a gentle pat, the affectionate holding of hands while walking in the park, or a surreptitious exchange of smiles.

Children need to see their parents be affectionate with each other. Often we would cuddle and mug for the kids, and Kent would say to the children, "You know I love you a lot. But I love your mother more!" Of course, they knew that we loved them with all our hearts. But the message was, "We really do love each other. Love is at the center of our family. You are a result of love." Seeing tender physical affection between parents enhances children's security and subtly encourages them to practice loving, In fact, when we were humorously affectionate with each other, our children would crowd around for their share.

Affection isn't inspired by lectures, but rather by the daily modeling of simple acts of kindness between parents — voluntarily helping with the dishes, keeping promises, and the quick response "I'm sorry; will you forgive me?" when one has been wrong.

The discipline of family affection demands that if we want to build love in the family, we must begin with the obvious: love for God and love for each other. If this does not exist, or is waning, family love will be very difficult to build.

Communicating

Clear communication is essential to family affection. Once, while traveling in the family station wagon, our youngest son chattered on endlessly as he leaned forward over the front seat. He was wildly enthusiastic about each topic that popped into his mind — a sort of spirited, third-grade stream of consciousness. Finally we reached the limit of our endurance and said, "Carey, will you please be quiet!" He plopped back into his seat, utterly disheartened, and said, "But talking's my gift!"

Talking may not be everyone's gift, but communication is certainly to be at the center of the Christian life. "Be filled with the Spirit," says

God's Word, "addressing one another in psalms and hymns and spiritual songs, singing and making melody to the Lord with all your heart" (Eph. 5:18-19). Among the signs of the fullness of the Spirit is joyous communication. It is essential for parents who desire loving communication in their family to be filled with the Holy Spirit. If your life is not Spirit-disciplined, optimum family communication and affection will consistently elude you.

The nature of communication. Scripture tells us to speak the truth in love (Eph. 4:15). So we understand that our communication is to be characterized by truth. But speaking the bare truth, as wonderful as it is, is not enough. It must be done in love. It is possible to do what the Scottish call "speaking the truth unseasonably" — that is, without regard to timing or the feelings of another. Loving communication is a balm. As Proverbs 24:26 says, "Whoever gives an honest answer kisses the lips."

Where it begins. This kind of communication is best caught rather than taught. Logic tells us that if parents are not speaking the truth in love, the children will not do so either. Good communication demands an investment of time.

During our seminary years, when the children were all quite small, we had a royal argument one morning just before Kent's classes were to begin. We scarcely spoke on the drive to the seminary. We were furious with one another, neither willing to give in. After we parted, we felt even more wretched.

Later that morning we did something impulsive and reckless in respect to our budget. We borrowed fifty dollars (a lot of money in the early seventies) from a friend who volunteered to care for the children, and we took off for an overnight getaway. Filled with unexpressed frustrations, we drove in silence toward Laguna Beach. It wasn't until we smelled the Pacific air that we began to relax. And then for the next twenty-four hours we communicated! We returned to our children the next day with renewed perspective, better able to inspire affection. It was one of the landmark times in our life. Like all couples, we needed to invest time and work to properly understand each other.

Today we make a disciplined investment in communicating. We talk every day. And we don't just engage in "news talk" about the day's events. We speak the truth in love. On our days off, we have breakfast at one of our "secret places" outside our town, and there we usually talk first about our children, then church, and whatever else comes to mind. It may sound sentimental, but we are best friends — soul friends.

Good communication is essential for building affection in the family. But that alone will not achieve the goal of dynamic affection. Some specific principles need to be put into practice.

How to Build Family Affection

Over the years we have worked at creating an atmosphere that produces the attitude "I have the best times when I'm with my family. When I'm with them I feel safe, loved, secure, unique, appreciated, accepted, and respected. They like me, and I like them." Families who experience this automatically build the bond of affection.

The Discipline of a Dinnertime Routine

An obvious place to enhance family affection is at the table. That is the single best daily opportunity families have for all gathering together. In bygone days, meals together were the norm, but not today. In fact, many families *never* eat a meal together unless it's in front of the television or at a local fast-food emporium. The frantic pace that most modern families keep rarely allows for a relaxed time devoted to the sole purpose of eating and conversation. We encourage you never to surrender that choice time, for it is an unsurpassed opportunity to build family life.

Making mealtime what it ought to be takes disciplined energy and thought. To begin, someone must take responsibility for preparing the meal. This means thinking ahead, planning menus, shopping for the necessary ingredients, learning to understand and follow recipes, and of course the *very* obvious: Someone must know how to cook, which is not always the case in our microwave world. It also requires time management — organizing everyone's schedule so that all are present when dinner is ready. It means setting the table and cleaning up afterwards. Mealtimes don't just happen — they must be planned. In a word, they are hard work. Yet without such discipline, no family will ever experience this positive, daily, affection-building time.

But effective mealtimes must involve more than consistent good meals if they are to build family affection. They must have a cheerful, positive atmosphere. And here the responsibility rests entirely on the parents. Parents must work at leaving their pressures and professional concerns outside the dining room and giving individual attention to their family. When the family meal is approached with gratefulness and appreciation for its provision and preparation, it will come to be anticipated as the best time of the day — "We're together! It's so good to be with my family."

Television can be the single most destructive factor in developing a positive mealtime atmosphere. Having the TV on means that the family will have to talk above another conversation, if indeed they do talk. Television will raise the noise level of the meal several decibels. TV also creates distracted half-conversations and minimizes eye contact. Similarly, if you find that the phone is constantly ringing at dinnertime, turn it off for half an hour.

Of course, families with tiny children should not have unrealistic expectations about mealtime, for it will rarely be idyllic. Neither should they be discouraged by the ordinary behavior of their young children. Mealtimes with young children are necessarily times of training. Children are establishing good eating habits, mastering the ability to hold a cup, and learning the proper use of a knife and fork. They are also learning how to participate in conversation, to be polite, to not interrupt, and to not talk with their mouth full. A major challenge during these early years is to not allow mealtime mishaps to ruin the atmosphere but instead to end the meal on a positive note.

Cultivating conversation. As children grow older, conversation becomes an increasingly important part of the mealtime. This is where issues will be discussed and opinions formed. But children have to be taught how to engage in intelligent, congenial exchange.

We discovered that teaching children to properly communicate begins early. Talk to your babies and preschoolers. Carry on conversations with them even when they cannot answer. Don't suppose that because they cannot talk back they don't comprehend what's going on. Include them in conversations by directing comments to them, speaking their name. Teach them to look you in the eye when you're speaking to them or they to you.

As they get a little older, let them know that you value their opinions: "What color place mats do you think we should use tonight?" or "Which flower do you like best?" Then begin to help them to value each other's ideas, first by teaching them not to interrupt each other. If a child wants to break into a conversation, instruct him to put his hand on your arm. The gentle touch will silently alert you to the fact that the little person next to you has something to say. We found this helped us not to overlook children who were patiently waiting their turn to speak. It also helped them establish the habit of self-control.

Once children have developed some basic conversational skills, mealtime is a perfect place to cultivate the open exchange that is so essential to family affection. Here are some disciplines that foster family conversation:

1. *Ask questions.* When our children began school, one of our common questions was "How was school?" Invariably it got a one-word answer: "Fine." So we replaced the question with a two-part question, "What was the best thing that happened to you today?" And then later, if necessary, "What was the worst thing that happened?" Usually that would get conversation going.

2. *Listen.* Children, even little ones who are barely articulate, can tell if you're listening to them. Our grandson Jamie let his mother know when he discerned she wasn't "with him" by climbing into her lap, taking her face in his hands, and saying, "Mommy, look in my eyes." So we must maintain eye contact and concentrate on following their reasoning.

3. *Show interest.* It is also important to show an interest in everyone's opinions and to encourage an exchange of ideas. Most children, with just a little encouragement, will attempt to participate in a family exchange. Once our two-year-old, in an attempt to compliment the cook, said, "Mom, that was malicious!" His comment has become one of our family codes — an affectionate way to say thanks for dinner.

4. *Be positive.* Conversations around the table with teenagers beginning to grapple with issues need not be unpleasant. Hear them out, and don't be threatened if they voice opinions contrary to what you want them to hold. Exercise self-control, and practice the proverb, "A soft answer turns away wrath" (Prov. 15:1). Dinnertime isn't the time to settle the world's problems or theological mysteries. But such topics must not be avoided either (see Chapter 4).

We never attempted to create a Pollyanna atmosphere, but negativism and criticism were minimized. The table was the place for stories, humor, recalling happy memories, and celebrating when one of our children passed a test or won an athletic event. The table was the place to sing and to laugh — even to fall off your chair in laughter. At the table we all shared the defeats of the day as well as the successes. If someone failed a test, lost a soccer game with his clumsy kick, or was overlooked for a part in the school play, the ache belonged to all of us. But shared mealtimes also provided the opportunity to restore perspective. A kind word of sympathy, a witty comment regarding the ineptitude of those unable to recognize the "genius" in a family member, and an encouraging word all engendered affection.

The Discipline of the Family Vacation

Family vacations were at the heart of building the Hughes clan's affection, and though our small salary in the early years left little to spare, *we made disciplined investment in family vacations.* One very special vacation happened because of Barbara's audacious determination. Deciding that we ought to have a great vacation on famous Balboa Island, Barbara and another young mother collaborated in producing plaster plaques, decorated and inscribed with Scriptures, which they persuaded some Christian bookstores to market. With the initial proceeds in hand, they contracted to rent the biggest available rental on the island — a beautiful five-bedroom house on the bay. They sold just enough plaques to pay for everything. And we had two weeks on the bay with our own beach and private sixty-foot dock, just like our movie star neighbors. What a time we had fishing from *our* dock, swimming and sunning, building sand castles, "burying" the fathers in the sand, walking barefoot on the hot sidewalk to town, where we all bought Balboa bars (what else!), and holding our own talent show in the evening before prayers and bed.

Why are vacations important? One reason, as we have been describing, is because vacations are fun. Family play is important for building camaraderie. Seeing parents play and being a part of family fun naturally strengthens a child's affection.

Another reason for family vacations is that they provide the *only* extended time in the year when kids have *both* parents to themselves twenty-four hours a day. This, along with the absence of professional pressures and distractions, allows the parents to give relaxed, undivided, unrushed attention to those who are most important in their life.

An all-family vacation also endows the family with mutual experiences that no one outside the family has. Vacations promote mutual discovery: "We found the old anchor together." Beaches and rock formations and architecture become ours. And all this contributes to the family lore that is repeated year after year in unconscious celebration of commonality.

Yet another reason for vacations is that lost opportunities cannot be recovered. A vacation forgone in 2004 cannot be taken in 2005 — at least not with the *same* children. Next year the children will be different — speaking new words, seeing the world through different eyes. You will not be able to buy that vacation back with blood or gold. You will not be able to influence your children next year the way you can this year.

Annie Dillard writes of a friend whose children had long been raised:

> The children were all very young, very small, and they were playing with buckets, and pouring water, and piling sand on each other's feet. I remember thinking, "This is it, now, when the children are little. This will be a time called 'when the children were little.'" I couldn't hear anything through the window; I just saw them. It was morning. They were all three blond and still curly headed then, and the sun was behind them.[3]

That is the way it will be for you before you know it!

Lastly, vacations are important because they make a disproportionate contribution to the treasury of positive family memories that are so crucial in enhancing affection. They certainly have enriched our parental affection — as Kent celebrated in these lines written on a summer day at San Onofre beach:

> *The sea rhythmic*
> *in platinum*
> *and blue*
> *Our daughters' hair*
> *more beautiful*
> *than any*
> *jeweler's creation.*

If we had not insisted that all our teenage children (some soon to leave home) arrange their summer schedule for a vacation to the East, they would not have the memories of listening to Dad preach in Boston's historic Park Street Church on the Fourth of July, or the sound of muskets reverberating through the sanctuary from fusillades fired in the adjacent Old Granary Cemetery, or hearing the choir sing "America" (first composed in Park Street Church in 1832). Neither would they have the memory of joining the great throng in the evening on the esplanade to listen as John Williams conducted the Boston Pops in the *1812 Overture,* complete with booming howitzers on the Charles River, or spending the following week at Cape Cod in the sweet autumn of our family vacations.

The importance of family vacations in building affection is substantial. In order for your family to have such a benefit, you must do two things: Do some disciplined *investment* and *planning*. If you wake up the first day of vacation and say, "What should we do?" you might end up with a misadventure like that of a National Lampoon movie. Vacations can be the best experiences your family will ever have — if you properly invest. And what dividends you will reap.

The Discipline of Planning Special Times

Family memories do not *need* to be built exclusively on long-term vacations. Sometimes brief, spontaneous mini-vacations can have important results in developing family unity and affection. Here are two examples:

1. *Pajama rides.* We owe this idea to Dr. Bob Smith, venerable college professor and grand family man. This is how it worked one summer night: Shortly after the children were tucked into bed, we went to their bedrooms and shouted, "Pajama ride!" Robes and slippers back on, and pillows in hand, we drove to the local Dairy Queen and had a round of ice cream. Then, to doubly surprise them, we drove across town to the other Dairy Queen and announced, "Seconds!" The variations of a pajama ride are endless — a trip to the drive-in movie, a visit to Grandma and Grandpa's, a nocturnal dip in the lake — you name it.

2. *After-school hikes.* On occasion we picked up the kids from school and drove to a nearby forest preserve, where a couple of the children slipped on backpacks containing snacks, and we went for a hike.

The proverb "Necessity is the mother of invention" was certainly true in our case. We *had* to be creative in finding time for the kids because pastors never have weekends free. So an occasional hour before or after school was perfect. Now and then we even took our children out of school on Monday afternoons (our day off) for an outing to the beach.

Mutual Interests

Our boys are fishermen by both natural inclination and parental design, for common interests are good for family affection. They were infected with the blessed virus early, when Kent carefully exposed them to some catching experiences. Over the years, fishing has spawned lengthy conversations about strategy and equipment, hours in the boat together, and one famous expedition (well, famous with us!) to the wilds of northern Ontario — plus endless fish stories, which Grandpa and the uncles now tell to the grandchildren to spread the same divine contagion.

Mutual interest builds affection, whether it's soccer, animals, collecting stamps or beetles or books, or a shared interest in art or the performing arts. Our children have broadened our interests to include everything from cars and metal detectors to gymnastics and ballet.

Wise parents know this and look for a common interest or adopt their children's interests as their own.

Uniqueness

We had once gone out to dinner at a casual Mexican restaurant, La Esquina. Waiting for our meals to come, our daughter Heather alternately arched and lowered her eyebrows, left-right, left-right, producing the illusion of a caterpillar crawling across her forehead. We were amazed. All of us in turn tried, but we discovered that we could raise only one eyebrow or both together. One thing led to another, and we found that each person had his or her unique facial muscle acrobatics. One could flare his nostrils, another could wiggle his ears, while still another could curl her tongue. By the time our meals arrived, we were exhausted from laughter. We were also fascinated with the amazing differences we possessed. Today, when we are in the mood, the old exhibitions sometimes return. Heather, thankfully, hasn't joined the circus!

True, our individual habits, expressions, and idiosyncrasies can annoy each other. But they also provide the stuff for endearing us to each other. They are the things that cause us to exclaim, "Good old Bob!" "That's Mary!" "You know Fred; that's the way he's always been." Families that learn to appreciate their points of uniqueness and to chuckle at their idiosyncrasies pull together in affection rather than apart in irritation.

Our La Esquina experience as *gringos locos* was supremely sane and a perfect instance of how we can ride our differences to endearing affection.

Nicknames

As we noted earlier, Phyllis McGinley was right in saying that happy families have a personal treasure of domestic humor that is not necessarily witty, and may even be incomprehensible to outsiders. Winston Churchill's family certainly did. His biographer, William Manchester, records that every family member had an endearing animal name. His beloved Clementine was "Pussy Cat," Marigold was "Duckadilly," Mary was "Mary the Mouse," and all their children together were "kittens." Manchester provides a glimpse of their domestic exchange:

> His home was an independent kingdom, with its own language. "Wow!" one of them would say in greeting another. When Churchill entered the front door he would cry: "Wow!" and his wife would call back an answering "Wow!" Then the children would rush into his arms and his eyes would mist over.[4]

The Hughes family has also developed its own domestic vocabulary, though not as eccentric as the Churchills'. Each child has several nicknames used only in the home, and we use some cryptic family phrases that would certainly confound the uninitiated. The point is this: We cannot say our children's nicknames without *feeling* a sense of love. Their very use engenders affection.

Fathers, leave your self-conscious masculine dignity outside the home. You will never be more a man than when tenderly addressing your family in endearing terms.

Many families have their own versions of songs that would be painfully embarrassing if used outside the home but are sources of affectionate in-house humor. When our children were young, they pestered their mother for this song, sung with a mock operatic falsetto to the tune of Rodgers and Hammerstein's "I'm in Love with a Wonderful Guy":

> *I'm in love with Richard Kent Hughes,*
> *He's my hero, he's Tarzan, I'm Jane.*
> *Since I met him, my whole life has changed,*
> *but I love him just the same.*
> *First came Holly, Heather, then Kent,*
> *Carey a little late—*
> *It gets exciting around our house*
> *every Sunday morning at eight!*
> *I'll listen to sermons ten times*
> *if I must—*
> *As we go through life, to heaven or bust!*
> *This song's dedicated to Patriarch Hughes.*
> *I'm in love,*
> *I'm in love,*
> *I'm in love,*
> *I'm in love,*
> *I'm in love with a wonderful guy!*

The home is the place to be sentimental, corny, even weird for the sake of affection!

Grandparents

Some grandparent friends of ours told this story about their grandson who lives in Taiwan, where his parents are missionaries. Little Nathan kept asking his parents if he could go over and visit one of his friends. His unusual persistence intrigued them. Finally they asked him why he so wanted to go to his friend's, to which he replied, "Because they say they have grandparents over there." The little guy's bond of affection with his own grandparents had him convinced that it must be wonderful to be anywhere grandparents are!

Wise parents who wish to enhance familial bonds will do their best to keep up the communication with grandparents and spend time with them if possible. Few things can be more elevating to family than loving affection extended across generations.

FOOD FOR THOUGHT

Why is love for God a necessary foundation for family affection? What does 1 John 4:8, 19 contribute to this subject?

Why is it important for children to know that their father and mother love each other? Is this the case in your home?

What role do having mealtimes together play in maintaining family affection?

What vacations will your children remember most fondly? What vacations would you still like to have that may have the same result?

What special times together has your family enjoyed? Should these be spontaneous or planned?

3

Discipline of
Starting Family Traditions

Kenneth Hansen, cofounder of ServiceMaster Corporation, claimed that it is important for every family to have traditions that are unique to itself. Our family has a Mother's Day tradition that, as best as we can figure, goes back about thirty-five years. It began with a Saturday powwow with our little girls, Holly and Heather, which in a few years included our boys, Kent and Carey. At this secret meeting, Dad agreed to buy strawberries, real whipping cream, and shortcake. The children agreed (with Father's help) to prepare the sumptuous surprise and elegantly serve it on the family's plastic plates to Mother in bed on Mother's Day.

The first couple of times, Dad assisted the children, but after that, they were on their own. In those early years, Mother's Day saw beautiful little girls and scruffy little boys "surprise" their mother with strawberries sublime, present her with their homemade cards, and then watch in unabashed admiration as she tasted the feast.

The children changed over the years. The girls became graceful women and the boys deep-voiced men. The plastic plates became china. But the Mother's Day feast and the loving admiration remained the same.

Strawberries in bed for Mother didn't just happen; it was the result of the conscious cultivation of tradition and memory in the Hughes family. The first secret powwow was Dad's idea, but after that the tradition belonged to the kids.

But why this disciplined emphasis on tradition and memory? Because of the rootlessness of today's culture. The contemporary world's post-Christian mind-set, its confusing pluralism, its broken families, the high rate of divorce, and the nomadic mobility of so many have produced a generation without memory or tradition. And frankly this is where many Christian families are — especially if they have not come from Christian backgrounds. These Christians feel rootless, alien, and insecure. This is sufficient reason for every Christian family to take conscious and disciplined measures to cultivate tradition and memory.

But there is an even more compelling reason. Namely, God's Word dramatically recommends that all believing families cultivate both spiritual memory and spiritual traditions to commemorate and celebrate God's goodness.

The following scriptural advice, put to work, will go a long way toward building secure families with a sense of solidarity with the past and the future.

THE DISCIPLINE OF KEEPING MEMORIES ALIVE

A stupendous miracle took place the instant the priests bearing the ark of the covenant set foot in the Jordan River. The waters stopped in one great, swelling heap nineteen miles upriver, leaving a barren riverbed all the way south to the Dead Sea. For hours the Israelites crossed in a broad, dusty swath until the rear guard of forty thousand warriors passed in full battle array (Josh. 3:15-17).

All Israel stood on the west bank, watching as twelve select men solemnly descended the banks and approached the ark. Then, kneeling at the priest's feet, each pried a stone from the river bottom and began a reverent procession up the west bank, through the waiting people, and across the plain to Gilgal (which means "the reproach has been rolled away"). There the twelve stacked their rocks to form a crude mound. To the symbol-oriented Israelites, the significance of the twelve stones was easily understood. They were *stones of remembrance*, placed as a visual reminder of God's great delivering power. Very likely, as Israel celebrated into the night, Joshua returned to observe, by the flickering light of their fires, the mound of stones. And as he gazed, he again and again ran his mental "tapes" of the day. God had done it! God was with him!

Significantly Gilgal, the place of remembrance, became the command headquarters for conquering the Promised Land. The stones of remembrance became a source of perpetual remembrance for Israel. God's command to Israel through Joshua was to let the stones

> *be a sign among you. When your children ask in time to come, "What do those stones mean to you?" then you shall tell them that the waters of the Jordan were cut off before the ark of the covenant of the* LORD. . . . *So these stones shall be to the people of Israel a memorial forever.*—Joshua 4:6-7

The stones of remembrance were not Joshua's idea, nor that of any man. They were erected in response to God's direct command, evidently because *God considers remembering essential to spiritual health*. In fact, remembrance is also given as the precise reason for instituting the Passover (see Exod. 12:21-27).

Thus we must conclude that building memorials (remembering the things God has done for us) is of the highest importance in personal spiritual formation and in raising children. It is imperative that we make disciplined attempts to preserve the memory of the great things God has done for us.

Over our nearly three decades of childrearing, the Hughes family has collected a considerable treasury of spiritual remembrances. A typed list fills several pages.

One of our stones was collected at Christmastime many winters ago when our pet-loving children were small. We were pastoring a newly planted church, and money was tight. The situation worsened when our English bulldog, Precious, had to have an operation. And everything hit bottom when we all returned from caroling one night to find our tomcat, Prudence (feline gender ignorance), near death due to a run-in with a car or a baseball bat. To survive, Prudence would have to undergo surgery, which would take all the money we had saved for our children's presents. So we put it to the children: It was the operation and no Christmas presents, or presents and no Prudence. Without hesitation, they chose Prudence.

But they also got a memorable Christmas — because someone far away, who knew nothing about our situation, sent us a check cheerfully designated "Christmas presents only." So we had our bandaged Prudence and Precious and presents too.

Our children, and their parents, have never forgotten that. It has become a stone of remembrance of the love and graciousness of God.

Another treasured spiritual memory came to us all through our youngest son's experience after we had saved and bought him a state-of-the-art "dirt bike." It was really quite spectacular, and our son was the envy of the neighborhood kids. Then it disappeared — stolen from our front yard. In Southern California, that undoubtedly meant the handlebars went one way, the wheels went another, and the frame was repainted. It was gone. But we prayed, and our son fervently prayed, that God would save his bike.

A month later, while driving on a busy boulevard, we glanced to the side of the road, and there was his bicycle, lying abandoned but in perfect shape! As we excitedly loaded his bike into the back of the station wagon, our son's first words were, "God has answered my prayers."

The benefits of a store of spiritual memories are substantial. They build spiritual muscle. In his second letter to the Corinthians, Paul remembers how God delivered him from death when he thought it was all over. Then, steeled by his memory, he adds that God "will deliver us. On him we have set our hope that he will deliver us again" (1:10). Families with a store of spiritual memories will be better equipped for tough times.

Spiritual memories also build security, as the psalmist testified: "I have remembered Thine ordinances from of old, O Lord, and comfort myself" (Ps. 119:52, NASB). And, of course, spiritual memories build the solidarity of the family because experiences of blessing and deliverance enhance our sense of togetherness and of mutual investment in each other's lives — and thus of our eagerness to give support to each other through thick and thin.

How to Build Stones of Remembrance

So then, how do we go about building a family treasury of stones of remembrance?

Recalling Memories

Set aside some time alone to read Joshua 4, and then ask God to help you recall appropriate memories. None of us has something as dramatic in our life as the parting of the Jordan. But all of us have some remarkable memories of, for example, God providing for us, answering a prayer, or working things out.

Recording Memories

Inspired by Joshua 4, one of the families in our church made a book entitled *Stones of Remembrance*. It has become a family centerpiece — open to all and continually growing. Others have used a family Bible or their own study Bible to record their memories. Whatever your preference, simply do it.

Modern technology has provided us with some remarkable means for chronicling God's workings in our families through tape recorders and video cameras. Get Mom and Dad or Grandma and Grandpa together, and record your family's spiritual oral history. Very likely, amazing revelations will come out because God is intimately at work in every one of his children's lives. What a spiritual treasure you will be creating not only for your family, but for potential generations to come.

Sharing Memories

Birthdays provide rich times for parents to reminisce about God's provisions or even miracles in their children's lives. The holidays — especially Christmas, when the relatives are together — provide another opportune time for sharing stones of remembrance. Years ago one of the families in our church began to attach a memory to each of their Christmas tree ornaments; so when they decorate the tree they spend the evening remembering God's goodness over the years.

THE DISCIPLINE OF ESTABLISHING AND PERPETUATING TRADITIONS

Memory and tradition naturally overlap. Tradition enhances remembering. But despite the overlap, they are not the same. Memory *recalls* God's goodness, whereas tradition *celebrates* the goodness of God. Just as God's

Word demanded memory as indispensable for spiritual health, it also commended tradition as essential to spiritual well-being.

The great emphasis on tradition is dramatically underscored by the amazing fact that after the initial mandatory *10 percent Lord's tithe*, which supported ministry, a second mandatory *10 percent festival tithe* was demanded from God's people and went for annual celebrations of God's goodness through feasting with one's family and friends (see Deut. 12:10-11, 17-18). The purpose of the festival tithe was to build religious celebration and mutual community among God's people. Think of it — 10 percent of all Israel's income was set aside to celebrate, to give thanks for God's goodness. Astonishing.

What does this personally mean to us who are not under the Old Testament economy? The huge outlay of resources to celebrate God's goodness, feasting with one's family and friends, tells us what God values, and a significant part of our time and resources should be invested in our family's regular celebration of God's goodness to us.

Christian Holidays

Applying the spirit of the festival tithe to the Christian family demands that we make the most of the great events of the Christian traditions, Christmas and Easter. The Hughes family has done this with gusto. As we share some of our family traditions with you, it must first be understood that the greatest focus of our celebration has been through our church, which has a rich Advent tradition with numerous services apart from Sunday morning. Passion Week is also enriched with multiple services on Good Friday. We believe that the church is a fundamental vehicle for celebrating God's goodness — and that is where your concentration ought to be.

But beyond the organized celebrations of the church, much can be done through traditions in the home. Family traditions can resonate with the festival spirit in commemorating God's goodness.

Advent. Early on, we began the tradition of lighting the candles of Advent, a ritual that emphasizes self-examination in preparation for the two comings of Christ, first in the Incarnation and second in final judgment. The highlight of our children's days was the progression of nightly Scripture readings and the relighting of each candle.

We coupled this Advent tradition with a Jesse Tree — a barren branch symbolizing that Christ came from the root of Jesse (i.e., in the Davidic line) and that he grew up like a tender shoot from dry ground (Isa. 53:2). Each evening one of the children had the privilege of placing on the tree a construction paper ornament reminding us of a prophecy about Christ while the appropriate Scripture was read. It would be misleading to give the idea that we did this every evening without fail and that the children were always angelic acolytes. We recall a few fights about whose turn it was and tears when little fingers got too close to the flame. But imperfect as we were, these traditions wonderfully enhanced our children's Christmas focus. And we cherish the memory of their beautiful, candlelit faces, luminous with a curious combination of impatience and wonder. (Extended instructions are given in the appendix on pages 161-188 as to how our church families use an Advent tree.)

Christmas. Decorating the Christmas tree is a big deal for most families, and we made the most of it. Mom would bake, filling the house with the aroma of gingerbread and spiced cider. Then after Dad put the lights on the tree, Mom would direct the decoration, narrating the progress with the significance of many of the ornaments: the tinfoil star atop the tree made by hand years earlier because we had no money for ornaments, the plastic wreath given to Dad by a lonely little boy on his soccer team, and so on. There were the usual irritations — lights that wouldn't work, spilled cider, and sometimes even short tempers — but that's not what everyone remembers. Today our grown children all want to make it home to share the ritual, *our* ritual, of decorating the family tree.

When we moved from L.A. to Chicago, we began the tradition of a Mexican feast on Christmas Eve to remind us of our California roots! *Feliz Navidad!*

Christmas Day itself always began with the first child to awaken singing:

> *Good Christian men, rejoice*
> *With heart and soul and voice,*
> *Jesus Christ is born today,*
> *Jesus Christ is born.*

As that single, sleepy voice awakened the others, they were to join in the singing until all were singing in unison. Only then could they get out of their beds and meet us at the Christmas tree, where we were singing the same song with heartfelt zeal. We use the word *zeal* because we want to encourage those of you who think this is possible only for "musical" people. We were so musically ignorant that when we started this tradition, we actually taught our children the song incorrectly because it was a carol we weren't that familiar with — we simply liked the words. (The full, correct text is given in the appendix on page 189.)

Can these little things mean much to the children? We found out when Heather and her husband, Jeff — just married December 13 and fresh back from their honeymoon — crept into the house Christmas morning before anyone else was up and began the traditional song. We all still sing it the wrong way, but it doesn't matter — God hears our hearts.

There is no doubt in our mind that household Christmas traditions, thoughtfully used, have enlarged our family's celebration of the goodness of God.

Easter. Easter, the other great Christian holiday, is greeted in our family with the Eastern Orthodox salutation "Christ is risen!" which brings the response "He is risen indeed!" Apart from our worship services, we also periodically celebrated the Passover with several other families, using a Christian seder. (See the appendix on page 191 for a list of resources to help you plan a Christian Passover celebration.) Easter Sunday, with its repeated Orthodox greetings and triumphant resurrection services, was always capped with a meal of roast lamb. When our children were small, the family Easter egg hunt featured a special find — a tiny lamb — as a reminder of "the Lamb of God, who takes away the sin of the world!" (John 1:29).

A Word About Feasting

If, as a family, you give to God's work in accordance with the biblical directives, and especially at holidays give attention to the poor, you should have no reservations about feasting. The festival tithe of ancient Israel has established the principle of feasting in celebration of God's goodness as important to family spiritual life. Some of the guidelines we used may be of help to you in enhancing your table. They are *worship, sameness, sharing,* and *hospitality.*

Typically, our worship at the table has included Scripture, prayers, and a hymn. For example, Christmas dinner is preceded by the reading of Luke 2, a hymn such as "Joy to the World," and prayer. Similarly, when we gather at the Easter table we read from an Easter narrative (John 19, Matthew 28, Mark 16, or Luke 24, or perhaps 1 Corinthians 15) and then sing an Easter hymn, such as "Christ the Lord Is Risen Today," and pray. Thanksgiving, though not a religious holiday per se, is intrinsically religious for the Christian, and we have made the most of it in worship with the reading of Governor Bradford's Thanksgiving Proclamation or a Puritan prayer, some Thanksgiving Scriptures, then prayer followed by the doxology. (Both the Thanksgiving Proclamation and the Puritan prayer are given in the appendix on pages 195 and 197.)

We have come to realize that consistency, not innovation for innovation's sake, is important. So we have established traditional entrées: turkey at Thanksgiving, tamales and enchiladas on Christmas Eve, prime rib at Christmas, and lamb at Easter. Predictable aromas, especially as they are associated with regular family celebration, enhance the anticipation of the event and more importantly build a sense of continuity and security — which is so important in this changing world.

We have found that our attempts at spiritual discussion at the table around the theme of the celebration have ranged from the sublime to the ridiculous. So much depends on who is there, the guests, the ratio of children to adults, how some are feeling, and quite frankly, the personal dynamics before coming to the table. One grouchy teenager can skew everything. Also, awkward attempts at "sharing" at the wrong time can put everyone off. Nevertheless, we have learned that if we do not prepare for spiritual discussion, it very likely will not happen. So we both come with starter questions in mind, and we wait for the right time to inject them. Sometimes it just doesn't work. But when it does, the result can be sublime.

The Scriptures call us to be hospitable (Rom. 12:10-13), and we have found that our traditional feasts are perfect opportunities to heed the call. Besides, hospitality is implicit in Old Testament directives about feasting:

> You shall eat [the offerings] before the LORD your God . . . you and your son and your daughter . . . and the Levite who is within your towns. And you shall rejoice before the LORD your God.—Deut. 12:18

Students away from home, singles without family nearby, and the elderly are all ideal people to invite. One year we hosted an exiled Bolshoi ballerina, who insisted on baking a huge napoleon. The creation of the monster pastry (twenty pounds) paralyzed our home for the better part of two days. But what substance it became for family interest and humor. And we were enriched when Luba Bershadsky sat at our table and talked about her life in the gulag and the miracle that Christ had wrought within her. (She shared her story in the book *I Know His Touch*, published by Crossway Books, now out of print.)

Secular Holidays

Secular holidays fall into two categories: *relational* (birthdays, Valentine's Day, Mother's Day, and Father's Day) and *patriotic* (Memorial Day and Independence Day). The relational holidays offer focused opportunities to celebrate God's goodness through family. Birthdays, Mother's Day, and Father's Day were all special in our family, and we encourage you to develop your own way of celebrating these joyful times.

Birthdays. We have many birthday celebrations each year. Our tradition has been for the celebrant to choose the dinner menu and the cake he or she wants. The cake is always served on the same pedestal cake plate amidst a special prayer and individual appreciation from the family members.

Mother's Day and Father's Day. Fathers, have a powwow with your little ones in preparation for Mother's Day. You may begin with an Erma Bombeckian experience: "Dad, the dog's in the kitchen! Get his paws out of there. Mom has to eat that!" "Where's the chili sauce?" "Don't you dare bleed on Mom's breakfast!" But despite the rough spots, Mom's smile will make it worth it. You will also have the smile of God — for you are celebrating his goodness.

One Father's Day the Hughes children turned the tables on their dad and gave *him* a pajama ride. It had been a busy Sunday, and after arriving home from the evening church service, Mom persuaded Dad to go to bed early — at 7:00 P.M. She would bring him supper in bed. But no sooner was he tucked in than all four teenagers burst in, shouting, "Pajama ride!" And Dad was escorted to the station wagon, driven (in his pajamas) to the most public places in town and displayed, and then finally chauffeured to the home of some good friends, where he dined on his favorite foods — artichokes (which he calls "the celestial flower") and root beer floats and pretzels.

We need to use common sense in regard to memory and tradition. Neither will happen unless there is a disciplined resolve to do something about it. Our human, sinful tendency is to forget God's benefits. And if we make no disciplined effort, we will not fully celebrate God's goodness.

We must make the effort to collect our stones of remembrance and create our own memorials. We must arrange the traditions of our family life into cycles of celebration.

On Mother's Day 1992, our youngest son wrote a letter to his mother about those strawberry celebrations that started so long ago. He wrote of the symbolism, the deeper meaning behind the annual gift of strawberry shortcake in bed. Here is what he wrote:

"The Meaning of Strawberry Shortcake"

So what is this deeper meaning? Do the strawberries represent the sweetness that comes to my soul when I hear your laughter across the dining room table as I partake of one of your many scrumptious Sunday dinners? Or are they the fruits of encouragement and confidence you have given me through the years with your positiveness and constant assurance that if you were sixteen you would date me for sure!

Could the whipped cream, being that enough of it will make even the worst dessert taste good, be a picture of your tough motherly love bringing out the good in a little boy who burns down avocado trees? Or is it a picture of your tender love bringing a smile to the face of a boy whose soccer game just got rained out?

Lastly, is the shortcake a subtle allusion to a genetic quality you may have passed on to me, or is the cake a reflection of the daily nourishment you have brought to my life by your consistent and faithful walk with God?

Mom, I would say the strawberry shortcake means all these things and more, but most of all it means . . . I love you.

—Wm. Carey Hughes
Mother's Day, 1992

FOOD FOR THOUGHT

Why are "stones of remembrance" important to family life today? What do they accomplish? What are some of your family's stones of remembrance?

What are some ways your family can record special memories? Discuss this together, and make a plan to make it happen.

"Tradition celebrates the goodness of God." What traditions has your family begun in order to do this? What traditions would you like to establish?

Why is the observance of Advent, Christmas, and Easter so valuable for family life? How has your family done this? How can you do it better?

Does your family discuss Scripture and spiritual themes at the dinner table (or elsewhere)? How has this been a challenge? A blessing? How can this be improved?

SPIRITUALITY

4

Discipline of Cultivating the Soul

A barefoot kindergartner made her way across the brown, sun-dried lawns of an apartment complex — the kind built after World War II to house servicemen and their families. As she hurried along, the breeze parted her overlong bangs, revealing bright eyes made even bluer with anticipation.

Mrs. White had promised that every child who memorized the special Bible verses would receive a little book that told a story even though it contained no words. If she won the book, she would have a story she could truly read.

Sitting quietly with her friends, she was transfixed. Before her were the treasured books, each with a brown leather cover that neatly snapped shut, and inside were four felt pages — black, red, white, and gold. She had demanded that her older sisters read the verses over and over to her, as she hadn't yet mastered reading herself. At last her time came . . . and her memory did not fail. Her little heart beat ever faster as she recited the verses that went with each color: black, Romans 3:23; red, John 3:16; white, Isaiah 1:18; gold, John 14:2-3.

She could hardly believe it as she held her tiny treasure and opened the pages as the children sang in unison:

> *Once my heart was black with sin,*
> *until the Savior came in.*

His precious blood, I know,
has washed it whiter than snow.
And in his Word I'm told,
I'll walk the streets of gold.
Wonderful, wonderful day!
He washed my sins away.

Barbara was that little girl. And along with the tiny prize, she received Christ as her Savior. Although she was only six years old, she understood clearly that now she had a heavenly Father who was preparing a place for her in heaven and that he had sent his only Son to die for her sin. From that day to this, she has never doubted that God is with her. Her conversion personally validates for us the immense spiritual capacity of children.

Jesus' words, "Let the little children come to me and do not hinder them, for to such belongs the kingdom of heaven" (Matt. 19:14) elevate and celebrate the faith and spiritual potential of children.

A Gallup poll taken during the 1980s beautifully corroborates Jesus' words. The statistics are that eighteen out of twenty people who come to Christ do so before the age of twenty-five. At age twenty-five, one in ten thousand will become Christians. At thirty-five, one in fifty thousand. At forty-five, one in two hundred thousand. At fifty-five, one in three hundred thousand.

Parents, we must believe in our children's spiritual potential.

As young parents, we were absolutely convinced of this, though there were many times we wondered if our prayers, teaching, example, and close attention were accomplishing anything. There were times when we wondered if what our little ones needed was an "exorcism" rather than discipline!

For example, when our youngest son, William Carey (note the missionary name!), was seven years old, Barbara was straightening his sock drawer and found his "stash" — a used beer can stuffed full of cigarette butts and a plastic bag, neatly folded shut, chock-full of the same! While it didn't take much imagination to figure out what our son was doing with this cache, Barbara could hardly wait to hear his explanation.

Carey arrived at the door sweaty and eager to be on his way back out to play.

"Yeah, Mom, what do you want?" Then he saw the opened drawer and its contents, and his eyes widened with guilt.

"William . . ." Barbara addressed him by his formal name. ". . . what are these items doing in your drawer?" In the silence came the scent of what she can only liken to wet chicken feathers, a smell she loved because it was the aroma of our little boy at play. Usually it compelled her to swoop him up, hugging and squeezing him, laughing as she told him, "I love little boys and chicken feathers!" This time she resisted.

Avoiding her eyes, Carey responded, "What items?"

With some firm prodding, he then told how he and one of the church elders' sons rummaged through the Saturday night party trash in the dumpster of the community center where our church met for Sunday school — drinking what remained in the beer cans and stashing the cigarettes for later use.

Barbara was incredulous at the thought of these two "sons of the church" downing rancid beer dregs and puffing away in secret machismo. She didn't know whether to laugh or cry.

Her voice rising, she said, "Carey, I'm really disappointed in you. What you have done is wrong!"

He responded, "It's not wrong. It's only wrong if I get caught."

Barbara's mind reeled. *This boy has been raised in a manse. He's already heard numerous sermons, not to mention hundreds of conversations at our table that touched on spiritual things and specifically on personal ethics like telling the truth (preschool and primary style, of course). And he actually thinks that a secret sin is OK if it remains secret.*

Times like these make parents despairingly question their actual influence in the lives of their children. They wonder if they are really getting through to their kids. But such jolts are not without benefit, for such events also remind us of our parental need of divine guidance and grace. No one can really know the mind of a child. No one except God can actually know what a child "hears" when his or her parent speaks. We thank God for caring enough about Carey's spiritual well-being that he led us to the discovery that gave us a landmark opportunity to teach a truth: that wrong is always wrong, whether or not it is discovered. At seven years of age, a very significant brick was added to the spiritual foundation of William Carey Hughes.

Today Carey is a spiritually sensitive, morally careful man (he is also a pastor, husband, and father) who is acquainted with his own capacities for good and evil — an acquaintance that began to be honed by this and similar events in his childhood years.

We must understand that on the road to spiritual maturity, most children bring us to the end of our own resources. We must also understand that all children have immense spiritual capacity. They can know Christ. They can ascend to remarkable spiritual heights, and they can also succumb to subtle delusion in their thinking. The way we raise our children must reflect our profound respect for their spiritual capacity because a proper appreciation of their spirituality will motivate us to work at their spiritual development.

Despite our inadequacies and mistakes, God has been faithful in helping us provide an environment in which all our children have spiritually flourished. Along the way, we have learned and practiced some essential soul-influencing disciplines.

THE DISCIPLINE OF PRAYER

Common sense tells us that the highest priority must be given to prayer if we hope to enhance our children's spiritual development. Yet this is where so many parents fail to measure up. Candid conversations have convinced us that many, perhaps even most parents' family intercessions are little more than perfunctory nods toward God: "Lord, bless Kaitlyn. Keep her safe from harm, and help her be a good girl and love you. We thank you for her. Amen." This is, of course, an acceptable prayer. But it isn't *much* of a prayer. It lacks specificity, like the generic missionary prayer, "Bless all the missionaries everywhere. Amen" — and it is about as effective. Effective intercession for our children requires that we pray with the mind engaged, in detail, with appropriate earnestness, and that both parents should often pray for their children together.

We are convinced that prayer commitments alone would revolutionize the spiritual development of the children of the church. This is why we will devote a full chapter to explicit common sense in prayer (Chapter 5).

THE DISCIPLINE OF BEING A GOOD EXAMPLE

You cannot reasonably expect your child to develop a spiritual quality that you contradict by your behavior. Possession of a character quality is essential to communicating it effectively. And inner qualities are most often communicated subtly, by example, rather than by pronouncement or edict. Who you are is more important than what you say. Bottom line: The quality of your own spiritual life is of greatest importance to your child's spiritual development.

This was one of the most important insights of the Puritans on the subject of the family. Here is what two of them wrote:

> Precept without patterns will do little good; you must lead [children] to Christ by examples as well as counsel; you must set yourselves first, and speak by lives as well as words; you must live religion as well as talk religion.[1]

> Be sure to set good example before your children. . . . Other methods of instruction probably will not do much good, if you don't teach them by a godly example. Don't think your children will mind the good rules you give them if you act contrary to those rules yourselves. . . . If your counsels are good, and your examples evil, your children will be more like to be hurt by the latter, than benefited by the former.[2]

On a memorable Saturday morning, our four-year-old son Kent awakened us, fully dressed and ready to go. He had put on his dress shoes and Sunday sport coat and slacks. His hair was wet and awkwardly slicked back, and he had a pencil over his ear (business fashion) and a pocket New Testament in his jacket.

"Where are you going?" we asked.

"I'm going to tell the houses about Jesus," was his reply.

It was such a dear, sweet, childish thing to do, and we treasure the memory of that moment. We were, of course, charmed. We realized that our son was imitating us, because he had observed that our faith was a serious matter — serious enough that we worked at sharing it with others. Like father, like son. Flattered, we were also sobered, seeing the enormous effect our example had upon our son.

Evangeline Booth, who would one day take her parents' place as general of the Salvation Army, wrote: "Very early I saw my parents working for their people, bearing their burdens. Day and night. They did not have to say a word to me about Christianity. I saw it in action."[3]

Miss Booth could say, "My mother and father practiced what I preach."

It's frankly pathetic when parents demand a faith or a commitment from their children that they themselves do not possess. How well we remember from our years in youth ministry a parent coming to us distraught over the direction of his teenager's life. He would complain, "My son isn't interested in church. I've made him come, but he doesn't like it. Something is wrong here!" In his distress he directed his fury at the church and its youth program. But the truth is, a pound of parent is worth a hundred pounds of preacher.

Practice what you preach. If you aren't disciplined in your behavior, it won't be long before your children will discover your inconsistency. And they'll want nothing to do with your hypocrisy. If you want your children to love church, *you* love church! Or, in matters of integrity, if you want your children to be truthful, don't lie. Don't tell your children to say you aren't home when someone you don't want to speak to calls. Pay your taxes. Return library books. Keep your promises. If you want your children to be kind and generous, be caring and magnanimous yourself.

Are we guaranteeing, then, that if you model these qualities, your children will automatically have them? Not at all. Common sense demands that we understand that our children are sinners just like us. But we are saying that you will not effectively communicate spiritual virtues that you do not yourself possess. Through your prayers and example, you can expect to see fruit in your children's lives — as we did in our daughter Heather in her concern for witness.

Heather and her father happened to be home alone one night when a nonbeliever came by the house to talk about his soul. As they conversed, Kent could smell the aroma of cookies baking, and soon young Heather appeared with a tray of milk and cookies. Kent's guest commented that the cookies were his favorite, and they went on with their conversation. As the man departed, Kent helped fetch his coat from the closet, and as the guest slipped his hand into his pocket, he felt the warmth of some neatly wrapped cookies and the note "Enjoy!" The man was overwhelmed. It seemed to Kent that more was communicated by Heather's hospitality that night than by all his nimble explanations.

Never forget in raising children that who you are is far more important than what you say. Next to prayer, the most important thing you can do for your child's soul is live a godly life. Don't make the mistake of focusing on methods if you haven't first focused on life.

THE SPIRITUAL DEVELOPMENT OF CHILDREN

Spiritual formation needs to be grounded in common sense regarding development. Children's spiritual calendars vary greatly. The observable outward growth of their body makes such diversity clear. Some walk when they are eight months old, others at sixteen months. The same child so quick to walk may be slow in speaking, while another, scarcely able to scoot about, is forming sentences. Some shoot up tall and gangly as preadolescent giants, only to be dwarfed by some late-bloomer in high school. It is the same with spiritual development, though all children have remarkable spiritual capacity. A wise parent will be practical about his children's spiritual development. Some will sprout early, while others destined for equal or greater spiritual growth will grow later, according to their own mysterious interior clocks.

We must be concerned about spiritual growth without rushing it. We are aware of the trauma that can be caused by a parent who insists a child be potty-trained before he has bladder control or walk before he is able. But greater trauma is inflicted by parents who insist that their child "accept Christ" before he or she is capable of making such a decision. Joseph Bayly has rightly decried the bogus conversions anxious parents have perpetrated — especially when the child is told, "Now Jesus is in your heart, and don't let anyone tell you differently." Very well, *if* the child has truly trusted in Christ. But there can be literal hell to pay if the parent is wrong.[4]

Having said all of this, let's be very clear what the goal of our children's spiritual development must be: nothing less than a true conversion of heart and soul. The mere recitation of a prayer about "asking Jesus into my heart" won't accomplish that. Erwin Lutzer, pastor of Chicago's Moody Church, tells about his own experience of "asking Jesus into my heart again and again but never feeling any different." He says further that "it wasn't until I was told as a teenager that Christ paid the penalty for my sin against a holy God and I no longer had to carry that burden, that I had peace."[5]

It is important that parents are clear about the content of the gospel when they talk to their children about it. The gospel has bad news to tell as well as good news. The bad news is that people are born sinners by nature. Their actions likewise show their bent toward evil. Because of this, no one can earn ultimate favor with God. The good news is that God himself has provided the way of salvation through the atonement of Christ on the cross for all who believe in him. The means of salvation is repentance from sin and faith in Christ's atonement for that sin. Once people place their faith in the cross as the means of their salvation, the Holy Spirit enters them and enables them to do what is right. (See appendix on pages 197-199 for a clear biblical explanation of the gospel.)

This means that whether you are from a tradition that makes use of teaching aids such as the Westminster Shorter Catechism or regular Scripture memory, you must keep returning to essential items for salvation — namely, that we are hopeless sinners and that the cross of Christ is the only answer — that "Christ died for our sins in accordance with the Scriptures" (1 Cor. 15:3). You must progressively instruct your children as to how his death was "according to the Scriptures," meaning the Old Testament Scriptures as they are fulfilled in the New Testament's revelation of Christ's cross and resurrection. Understand again that if you yourself do not fully understand this, you will not be able to pass it on accurately to your children. A very readable explanation of the Cross is Leon Morris's celebrated book *The Atonement*. Also, you must never succumb to the wrong thinking that this is the responsibility of the youth group and Sunday school. True conversion of the heart and soul of your children is your God-given charge. The family is, as the Puritans said, a miniature church. (See appendix on page 159 for a list of aids to Christian education for use in the family.)

We need to add a warning: Don't manipulate your children. Parents, be very concerned about your children's spirituality, but don't manipulate them. Pray like crazy. Set a consistent example. Instruct your child in the essentials. As best you can, be sensitive to his or her spiritual development. But don't be a "nervous Nelly." *Trust God to work in your child's life in his own good way and time.* Relax.

ADDRESSING DOUBT

Paradoxically, doubt is a part of living faith, and most children will have their doubts. We were on vacation in the Rockies when young Kent, then twelve, was having doubts. After a morning of fishing with his father, he indicated that he wanted to talk about God. So that afternoon he and his father descended a ravine, settled under a pine tree because it was misting, and began to converse. His questions were about the existence of God. It is difficult to believe in a being you cannot see. Kent was asking questions many have but do not always feel free to ask. His father was answering the best he could, but not always to Kent's satisfaction. But their talk was long and good.

At last they prayed together and climbed out of the ravine, our son first. Kent startled his father by exclaiming, "Dad, look — two rainbows!" And sure enough, there were two distinct rainbows, separate from each other. Young Kent, thinking of Noah's rainbow, said emotionally, "It's a sign, Dad. One for you and one for me." For him, it was an affirmation of God's existence.

That is a treasured family memory, a memory our son fondly recalls, and an ongoing encouragement amidst the recurrent doubts that come to him, as indeed they come to us all.

Doubt is part of belief. As Oxford theologian Alister McGrath has said:

> Doubt is natural within faith. It comes because of our human weakness and frailty. . . . Unbelief is the decision to live your life as if there is no God. It is a deliberate decision to reject Jesus Christ and all that he stands for. But doubt is something quite different. Doubt arises within the context of faith. It is a wistful longing to be sure of the things in which we trust. But it is not and need not be a problem.[6]

McGrath suggests that we need to learn to be relaxed about doubt — and we emphatically agree. Building on this wisdom, we offer some suggested disciplines for dealing with your children's doubts as they grow in faith.

Don't get "Shook"

Parents who recoil in pious shock at their children's doubts make a crucial mistake. Hear them calmly. Objections like "How can you think such a thing?" or "That's blasphemous!" notify your child that rational discussion is out of the question and that you are not as secure in your faith as you would like to think. Be confident. After all, the historic faith can stand very well on its own.

Dialogue

Dealing with doubt requires that there be dialogue — a two-way conversation. Resist the parental impulse to lecture, a sure death to dialogue. Listen. And we mean truly listen, with consistent eye contact. Follow what your child is saying even if to you it seems illogical or boring. At the same time, never patronize. Listen intensely and patiently to an illogical argument or doubt, but then do not refrain from gently explaining what you believe and why. Also resist the compulsion to get in the last word. Last words rarely settle anything.

Don't Offer Bromides

Dismissing a doubt with a shallow remark — "If you want to think you came from a monkey, that's your privilege" — or answering with pious jargon — "Just trust, and you'll come to see it as I do" — is deadly. Your children can tell when you're being flip or speaking in clichés. Don't think you must have a glib answer for every question. In fact, admitting that you *don't* know something may have more effect in building a child's faith than a quick answer would. (See appendix on pages 241-245 for helpful answers to the most commonly asked questions about Christianity.)

Do Your Homework

The benefit of a questioning child is that he will drive you to do some healthy homework and thus become more articulate about your own faith. A doubting child can be the impetus to initiate some healthy conversations with your pastor and some enriching reading in areas like the problem of evil, biblical creation, the existence of God, and the authority of Scripture. Christian parenting is not for the mentally lazy — praise God.

Space

As you oversee your children's spiritual development, have the good sense to give them some space. Often anxious parents become so controlling and smothering that their claustrophobic children become crazed for space, eventually rebelling. Remember that the words *child* and *change* are virtually interchangeable. Everything is in flux: body, glands, persona, and mental processes. Because of this, children are often a bundle of contradictions. One of our teenagers spent a week alternately practicing his break-dancing moves to the heavy beat of his sound system and tenderly weeping as he read the poignant biography *A Man Called Peter*.

Understanding the need for space, we determined that we would say yes to as many things as we could while saving our no's for the truly important issues, and that we would be stringently biblical in deciding which was which. When Carey's soccer team went to the regional play-offs his senior year, each team member decided to have an ear pierced and don a team earring until the team either was eliminated or won the play-offs. Some parents — both churched and unchurched — objected, but we did not. We were not enamored with his studded ear, but we saw that it was not a biblical or moral issue and certainly not a sign of rebellion. We had the common sense to give Carey some space and save our no for something else. Today the earring is long gone, but the Lord still has our son's heart.

PARTNERING WITH YOUR CHURCH

To imagine that you can raise a godly child with little or no commitment on your part to the local church contradicts common sense, not to mention Scripture. Yet this is what many attempt today. Their "church" is a diet of Christian radio and TV programs and a few Christian books. For others, fueled by the consumer mentality, "church" is a perpetual shopping day. They attend one church for the worship service, send their children to a second church for its youth programs, and go to a third church's small group. So we have a phenomenon unthinkable in other centuries: churchless Christians. A vast herd of professing Christians attempt to raise Christian families without accountability, without discipline, without responsibility, living apart from the regular benefit of the ordinances.

Yet the common conviction of the church from ancient times to the present day is that if God is your Father, you must have the church as your mother. Lone Ranger Christianity should be unthinkable.

If you wish to see your children spiritually advance, you need to live out these disciplines of the church:

• You must commit yourself to a local expression of the church.
  • You must regularly attend its services of worship.
  • You must give of yourself to its ministry and leadership.
  • You must give of your resources for its support.
  • You must insist that your children attend with you. (You would never dream of allowing them to choose not to go to school. Is church less important?)
  • Youth group is not sufficient.

The local church was the womb that warmed our soul until it was ready for birth. The church fed us on the milk of the Word, providing us with many loving fathers and mothers. It stood with us when we presented our children to God, and it now mothers them. The local church has contributed much to our children's spiritual nurturing in the following areas:

• *Worship* — participation in corporate worship has educated them and intensified their adoration of God.

• *Education* — the church has helped us perform our duty to teach our children God's Word.

• *Friendship* — their life-changing relationships (their best friends, adults as well as peers) have come from the church.

• *Discipleship* — through the church's Bible school, club programs, and youth groups, they have been confirmed in the ways of God.

• *Mission* — their hearts have been enlarged by the church to reach out to the world.

The local church is God's provision for spiritual nurture.

Take this to heart: Your children may not fully become what they ought to be apart from *your* commitment to the local church — whether it be a house church or a large, multi-staffed church.

Have you been a church hitchhiker? Settle down — for the sake of your children's souls and your own.

THE DISCIPLINING OF CONSCIENCE

Scriptural logic tells us that we must nurture and educate our children's moral sense — their consciences — as part of spiritual development. Strangely, this is not in vogue in some Christian households, a perspective no doubt influenced by our culture's doctrinaire relativism, which insists that "right" and "wrong" are simply matters of perspective. Unduly swayed by such thinking, parents have suffered a loss of moral confidence, and thus are hesitant to command obedience to what is right. It is more common today to recommend a course of conduct because "it is best for you." The appeal is to self-love rather than right or wrong.

This is far from God's Word. For example, Paul commanded children to obey their parents, for this is *right* as opposed to *wrong*. A wonderful thing about appealing to conscience is that it exercises the conscience, thereby building moral muscle, an indispensable component of your child's spiritual formation.

Parents, have the good sense to insist that your children tell the truth — not so much because it is to their advantage, but because it is right. Their convictions to do right will make them aware of their inability to do so consistently and of their boundless need of God's grace and help. *No one is ever born again apart from a knowledge of sin and repentance.* So when you insist on kindness, obedience, giving, forgiving, and loving because they are right, you are helping move them toward a knowledge of their great need.

A conscience so disciplined, and by such discipline made clear, will equip your child to stand tall in this alien world. As Paul instructed Timothy, "So fight gallantly, armed with faith and a good conscience" (1 Tim. 1:19, NEB).

MOTIVATION

Spiritual logic informs us that, as in the rest of life, our fundamental motivations for cultivating our children's spirituality are of greatest importance. Wrong motivations are self-defeating. For example, some parents are motivated by what they see as the *advantages* of Christianity — namely, Christian civilities and some connections with the "good people" in the community, with a ticket to heaven tossed in. God forbid that their children take their faith too seriously and become "fanatics." Such motivations produce cultural Christians who are at best civilized and connected, but with no spiritual reality and no eternity in heaven.

Other parents are motivated by *appearances*. They want their children to become "spiritual" because it will make their parenting look good. Often this accounts for the lockstep demands some parents place on their children. They choose everything for their children, sometimes even their clothing, with an eye to impressing the Christian community. Such motivations produce external conformity while generating an inward rebellion that will ultimately take its toll.

The single most important motive for raising children is the *glory of God*, and that is where we must remain grounded. We must endeavor to instill in them a character that radiates God's glory. We must work to build in our children a life direction that wants nothing less than God's glory. We must toil to form a lifestyle that desires to "do all to the glory of God" (1 Cor. 10:31).

A life focused on God's glory will have glory for its own reward, for "then the righteous will shine like the sun in the kingdom of their Father" (Matt. 13:43).

Careful discipline regarding your child's soul will pay off. It must begin and end with disciplined prayer. That is the key. Along with prayer, you must discipline yourself to exemplify the qualities that you wish to characterize your child, understanding that spiritual growth takes time and is unique to each soul. Be a serious student of the Scriptures and the holy doctrines therein so you can teach your children.

Remember to give your child time and space to grow. Never neglect the discipline of regular family attendance at a good church. Always appeal to your child's conscience for the sake of his or her moral development and conviction of sin. And undertake all of your disciplines to the glory of God.

A final reminder is this: Spiritual nurture of children will thrive only if parents remind themselves continually of the primacy of the spiritual. There are so many family activities, so many opportunities that parents want to make sure their children don't miss out on, that it is easy to let the primacy of the spiritual erode. The Puritans were great on the subject of putting first things first, and here is what one of them said about priorities within a family:

> Before all, and above all, 'tis the knowledge of the Christian religion that parents are to teach their children. . . . The knowledge of other things, though it be never so desirable an accomplishment for them, our children may arrive to eternal happiness without it. . . . But the knowledge of the godly doctrine in the words of the Lord Jesus Christ is of a million times more necessity for them.[7]

FOOD FOR THOUGHT

Do children have the capacity to understand and believe spiritual truth, to come to Christ? How can we discern our children's state and help them develop spiritually?

What is the importance of parents' prayers for their sons and daughters? How specific should these prayers be? How specific are your prayers?

What are some unhelpful ways of dealing with your children's spiritual doubts? What are some better ways?

If your child asked you what the Bible is all about, could you answer in a sentence? If not, why not?

If your child asked you, "What is the gospel of Jesus Christ?" how would you answer? (See Appendix, "Two Ways to Live.")

5

Discipline of
Praying with Dedication

St. Augustine's *Confessions* reveals that his early life provided little hint of the great Christian he would one day be. From all indications, the brilliant young man would become a dissolute professional, probably in law or academia. As a seventeen-year-old student, he acquired a live-in girlfriend who shared his bed for a decade and bore him an illegitimate son. Intellectually, Augustine embraced not Christianity but the Manichean heresy, which smugly claimed to reconcile philosophy and religion. And at the age of twenty-three, while teaching rhetoric, he wrote a book with a title that today sounds very much contemporary — *On the Beautiful and the Fit*. Augustine was hardly a candidate for the church, much less sainthood.

But he had something special going for him — his mother Monica, a woman of immense faith and persistent prayer. She pursued him from North Africa to Rome (where he tried to give her the slip) and then to Milan, where he was soundly converted. The rest is treasured church history, for he became Augustine of Hippo, the greatest theologian of the early church.

Upon Monica's death, Augustine poetically expressed his grief to God: "I wept [for] my mother . . . the mother who for the time was dead to mine eyes, who had for many years wept for me, that I might live in Thine eyes."[1]

Monica's prayers for her son serve as a bracing example of the power of parental intercession. Indeed, the greatest single thing that parents can do for their children is to regularly offer loving, fervent, informed, detailed prayers on their behalf.

The responsibility of parental intercession is rooted in the oldest documents of the Bible. Significantly, the first chapter of Job informs us that when Job's children feasted, he would have them purified. Then Job "would rise early in the morning and offer burnt offerings according to the number of them all. For Job said, 'It may be that my children have sinned. . . .' Thus Job did continually" (1:5).

So we understand that from time immemorial, believing parents have regularly lifted their children before the throne of God in loving intercession. Certainly there are many other indispensable elements to Christian parenting, but prayer is of the utmost importance. As John Bunyan declared,

> *You can do more than pray*
> *after you have prayed.*
> *But you cannot do more than pray*
> *until you have prayed.*

Our Bible and common sense tell us it is absurd for Christian parents to read books about how to be better parents if they do not pray for their children. Yet some parents insist that their children attend church and Sunday school and youth group, memorize Scriptures, and attend Christian schools, while having no prayer life on their behalf. "Lord, I don't have time to pray. I'm too busy making sure my children have a Christian upbringing!" Sadly, this is exactly the way thousands of Christian parents live.

The advice we offer is not from the ivory tower, but from the car pool, the life of skinned knees, sticky telephones, and last-minute term papers. Busy as we were, we prayed. We must emphasize that prayer is not something we have mastered. Having the discipline to make time for prayer is a continual battle, and one that has not become easier with the years. But we do it.

THE DISCIPLINE OF HAVING A PRAYER LIST

A caution is in order here. Our advice may seem daunting, but the reader must remember that it comes from forty years of parenting (eighty in the aggregate)! Our advice is also very personal; it fits our unique blend of personalities. Therefore, it would be unwise for any individual or couple to embrace it uncritically. Better to read the chapter through and then prayerfully implement a few of the suggestions that will most directly enhance your parental prayers.

Experience has taught us that a prayer list is indispensable. Our own tendency to mental laziness in times of prayer, especially when we were tired, necessitated a list. A prayer list helps concentrate the mind and helps us recall the little things as well as the big. We found that when we did not have our lists, we would forget to pray for needs that we had presumed were impossible to forget. Likewise, prayer lists aid you in being more systematic in prayer, and they help monitor intercessory progress as requests are scratched off and added.

In explaining how to make a prayer list (which is a part of our larger prayer notebook), we have found that it is most helpful to present it all together. So our explanation will be as follows: first a description of our *prayer notebook*, which contains six divisions; second, an explanation of the fifth division, which deals with *petitions*; and third, our *family prayer list*, which is a part of the petition section.

Making a Prayer Notebook

Our prayer notebook is a small, five-by-seven-inch, three-ring, loose-leaf binder that has six divisions:

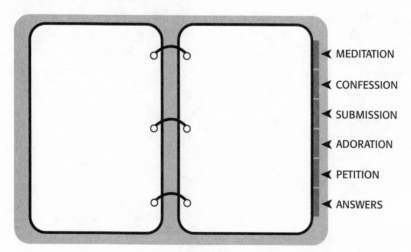

◄ MEDITATION

◄ CONFESSION

◄ SUBMISSION

◄ ADORATION

◄ PETITION

◄ ANSWERS

Sometimes we pray through the divisions from beginning to end. Other times we will utilize one or two sections.

The *Meditation* section lists the full texts of the Scriptures that we are presently meditating on and memorizing.

The section on *Confession* contains verses that instruct us regarding our sinfulness and the necessity of confession. We regularly read these Scriptures as an aid to confessing our individual sins.

Submission naturally follows confession. Here we also have the texts that deal with this subject and some prayers (some collected from others and those we have written) for submitting ourselves to God.

The *Adoration* section covers several pages and contains more collected material than we could use in several devotional times. It lists Scriptures, songs, and poetry that tilt the heart upward. (See the appendix on pages 201-204 for an extended layout of Scripture, songs, and poetry used under these first four divisions.)

The *Petition* and *Answers* sections naturally conclude our prayer notebook. The Petition section is of the greatest relevance to the reader because it contains the family prayer list.

Making a Petition Section

The Petition section is divided into two sections: *Weekly Petitions* and *Daily Petitions*.

The weekly petitions occupy four pages. Each of the pages provides a list to be prayed through once a week. We have four lists instead of one for each day of the week to allow for the inevitable missed days and also for flexibility in devotional routine. We also use Post-it® notes under each heading to allow for easy revision without redoing the entire page.

PAGE 1:	PAGE 2:	PAGE 3:	PAGE 4:
Ongoing III	World	Christian Leaders	Government Leaders —local
Others' Prayer Requests	U.S.A.	Pastors	—state —federal
Spiritual Warfare	Personal Life	Upcoming Ministries	Longtime Friends
Friends	Needed Personal Qualities	Vision	

A sample page is shown below.

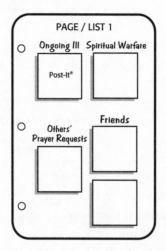

Next, our daily prayer list is concisely laid out over three pages. The daily headings are *Family, Staff, Ill, Grieving, Problems, Important Events, Ministries, Corporate Worship, New Believers, Missions.* Post-it® notes are also utilized under some of these headings.

Making a Family Prayer List

The family heading is naturally the most detailed part of the daily prayer section. We begin this section with two prayers originally prayed for the Ephesian church. We have modified them into prayers for family. Very often we preface our specific family petitions by praying one of these beautiful prayers.

> Ephesians 3:16-19 for the family: *Father, we pray that out of your glorious riches you will strengthen our children with power through your Spirit in their inner beings, so that Christ may dwell in their hearts through faith. And we pray that our children, being rooted and established in love, may have power, together with all the saints, to grasp how wide and high and deep is the love of Christ, and to know this love that surpasses knowledge — that they may be filled to the measure of all the fullness of God.*

> Ephesians 1:18-19 for the family: *We pray that the eyes of our children's hearts may be enlightened in order that they may know the hope*

to which Christ called them, the riches of Christ's glorious inheritance in the saints, and his incomparably great power for us who believe.

You will never err when praying God's words. Moreover, they will inform and enrich your subsequent prayers with the wisdom and cadences of heaven.

You may find it helpful, though certainly not necessary, to mount a small photo of each child followed by prayer headings and detailed petitions as shown below.

As we prayed through the headings for our preteen daughter, our prayers went something like the following:

Spirituality. "Lord, we pray for Heather, asking that she will truly understand and rest in what your Son has done for her. We ask that she will come to love you with all her heart and become a devoted Christian. Shape her life so that she will finish well."

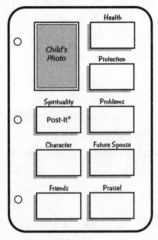

Character. As we recall, Heather had some trouble with deception and truthfulness. It wasn't chronic, but it concerned us. So we would pray: "And, Lord, help Heather to be truthful. May her conscience burn if she is deceiving us. Give us wisdom so that we will not overreact or be too lenient."

Friends. Anyone who has raised a daughter knows how difficult little girls' friendships can be and how they can dominate a child's existence. Also, peers can be so influential in development. We prayed for her friends, as well as the perpetual "mini-crises" that came her way.

Health. Loving parents have an abiding concern for their children's health. And if you have several children, it seems that one is always ill. So we regularly invoked our health concerns in great detail.

Protection. So much evil can befall children today, and so we fervently prayed for their protection spiritually, socially, and physically. Our prayers for Heather often were: "God, protect her from evil; guard her from demonic attack. Give her safety from the social temptations that come her way — the music, the peer pressure. Help her to stand tall. And, Lord, protect her from physical trauma. Shield her from molestation and abuse."

Problems. Sometimes this heading was bare. Other times it bore reminders of specific problem areas with which we were dealing.

Future spouse. From the time our children were babies, we prayed that if they were to be married, God would give them godly, loving spouses. We tell our sons-in-law today that we have prayed for them for three decades!

Praise! We always thanked God for each of our children, reciting what we so appreciated: "Thank you for her sweet spirit and cheerful heart. Thanks for your protection and for the good days she has been having. Amen."

COMMON SENSE ABOUT PRAYER

A few reminders are in order at this point. First, you may legitimately feel that you do not need such an elaborate prayer list. A simple version will do quite well. For example, a three-by-five-inch card with your children's names and minutely inscribed reminders can bring to mind the necessary information. Some of our friends have typed their lists, reduced them to small print on a copy machine, and then laminated the card with plastic so it can be easily carried in a wallet or purse.

Second, realize that you can of course pray without the list. Slavish use of a list will drain the joy from your prayers. Sometimes you should purposely pray for your family without the list, asking God to direct your spontaneous intercession.

Third, another tried and true method of domestic intercession is to take a pen in hand, list the name of your child, and briefly note your petitions as you go. This will help you to think your prayers clearly and to be focused.

The Discipline of Preparation and Work

Prayer is work, not a sport. It is not something that you do if you like, or devote spare time to, or do only if you are good at it. Prayer requires hard soul-labor, as Paul's challenge to the Ephesians eloquently attests:

> a. . . . praying at all times
>
> b. in the Spirit,
>
> c. with all prayer and supplication. . . .
>
> d. Keep alert with all perseverance,
>
> e. making supplication for all the saints. (Eph. 6:18)

This is not a call to pray if we feel like it. It is a call for spiritual sweat.

Consistency

Logic tells us that any effective prayer life must be regular and that we must strive for consistency. But clear thinking reminds us that we will sometimes miss our prayer times. Do not become discouraged at lapses, and do not succumb to the miserable thought that you have to "make up missed prayers." Sometimes our best planned days simply detonate. And on those occasions we do well just to fall into bed saying, "Lord, I'm tired! Amen." God is not a computer; he's a Father, and he understands. So wake up guilt-free, and try the next day — even if it, too, explodes!

Finding Time

Our busy world is inhospitable to prayer because it neither understands prayer nor allows time for it. We have to fight for prayer time.

Fathers who find it difficult to pray at home even when they get up early — because some sleepy-eyed little person invariably comes wandering in — can remedy the problem by leaving thirty minutes earlier for work and stopping in the parking lot of a donut shop or drugstore for half an hour of devotion and prayer. Working parents can sometimes utilize part of their lunch hour. But those at home with little children have no such opportunities. Obviously, there is nap time, and that can serve well if Mother has the stamina. However, she often needs sleep more than the kids do.

So some creativity is needed. One idea is to alternate days with a neighbor or friend in watching each other's children. This could free up an hour two or three times a week for devotions. Another way for the stay-at-home parent to carve out some devotional time is for the husband to provide his wife a free hour in the evening while "Momma gets away." Good sense demands that both husband and wife must assist each other if they are to have healthy prayer lives.

Length

It is a mistake to imagine that prayers must be long in order to be effective and pleasing to God. Martin Luther said:

> Look to it that you do not try to do all of it, do not try to do too much, lest your spirit grow weary. Besides a good prayer mustn't be too long. Do not draw it out. Prayer ought to be frequent and fervent.[2]

It is far better to have ten minutes of concentrated prayer than an hour in which one's mind wanders from Jerusalem to Timbuktu. A legalistic commitment to duration will inevitably torpedo your prayer life. Also, remember that we are challenged to pray as we go through the day. "Rejoice always, pray without ceasing," advises the apostle Paul (1 Thess. 5:16-17).

Praying Together

When Christian couples begin life together, they often share an idealized picture of domestic devotion. They imagine themselves leisurely reading the Bible together, discussing at length a rich devotional thought from Oswald Chambers, praying around the globe, singing together "It Is Well with My Soul," and dropping off to sleep in each other's arms as their Bibles slip to the floor. A few months of marriage inject a jolt of reality. And when children come, the couple begins to despair of ever finding time to pray together other than grace at meals.

But there is time for daily prayer if couples will go to bed at the same time and if they keep their prayers short. We have found that, aside from brief daily prayers together, an extended time for mutual prayer can reasonably be arranged once a week. For us, it has been on our day off, when we take a good hour or more together to pray about everything.

Common Sense About Answers

The heartwarming story of Monica, that blessed mother who assaulted heaven for the soul of her errant Augustine, challenges every Christian parent with the necessity and efficacy of disciplined intercession. But experienced praying parents also know their prayers do not guarantee that all will go smoothly in raising children.

The granite reality of this struck us hard during one of our children's senior year in high school. To be perfectly frank, we actually feared that all was lost. We wondered about the efficacy of prayer and our Christian commitment. It wasn't until the eleventh hour that the change came. Today that same child has solid commitment that has persevered through subsequent trials of remarkable intensity.

We parents must allow our concept of prayer to be shaped by scriptural reality, for then we will understand that our prayers are not tools with which to manage God. Rather, the opposite is the case, because God uses our prayers to manage us, to bend our will to him and brand our soul with his character. When parents truly pray for their offspring, their prayers bind both their soul and the souls of their children into a mystery that ultimately deepens the life of each.

Often the silence of God is a mute sign of a greater answer. Oswald Chambers explained:

> Some prayers are followed by silence because they are wrong, others because they are bigger than one can understand. It will be a wonderful moment for some of us when we stand before God and find that the prayers we clamoured for in early days and imagined were never answered, have been answered in the most amazing way, and that God's silence has been the sign of the answer.[3]

God hears the prayers of believing parents and delights to answer them in amazing ways.

The Holy Scriptures and the Holy Spirit call us to pray. We need to let the discipline of prayer be the ground of all our childrearing.

> *Prayer is the first thing,*
> *the second thing,*
> *the third thing.*
> *Pray therefore.*
> *Pray, pray, pray.*[4]

FOOD FOR THOUGHT

What does the example of Augustine's praying mother convey to you, generally and personally? Do you agree that praying for your children is the greatest thing you can do for them?

Do you agree that a prayer list is a great tool for effective prayer for your family and friends? Have you tried this? With what success? Are you using one now? Why or why not?

Do you find prayer enjoyable or work? What does Ephesians 6:18 teach us about prayer?

What does it mean to "pray without ceasing" (1 Thessalonians 5:17)? How can you do this (be as practical here as you can)?

Do you and your husband and wife find it easy or hard to pray together? How often are you doing this? What can you do, practically, to make this a habit?

6

DISCIPLINE OF
PURSUING FAMILY MINISTRY

The family is a wonderful means of evangelism, especially when children become school-age. We rejoiced in our good fortune when our daughter Holly became one of Mrs. Smith's kindergartners. Susie Smith was considered simply "the best." A tall woman in her mid-thirties, she was unusually graced with what the French call the *joie de vivre*. Mrs. Smith brimmed with joyous enthusiasm about life and teaching. And she loved her students.

When Mrs. Smith smiled, her eyes stretched wide like her mouth, so that for a bright second all you could see of her eyes was the sparkle. That smile and the warm cheer of her husky voice soothed the anxieties of students and parents alike. This winsomeness, along with her wholesome enthusiasm and creativity, made her a master teacher. And our shy little Holly loved Mrs. Smith.

Holly, nurturing soul that she was even then, often thought of Mrs. Smith and how nice it would be if she came to church — and could know Jesus. So every Friday Holly's guileless brown eyes engaged Mrs. Smith's as she asked, "Mrs. Smith, will you come to church this Sunday?" And every Friday Mrs. Smith answered, "Well, maybe." Every Monday, as Susie Smith tells it, our disappointed daughter said, "Mrs. Smith, you didn't come." At last it simply became too much for Holly's poor teacher to face, and she promised to come to church.

And so Susie Smith visited and then came again and again — for she had a deep, unfulfilled spiritual need that was finally met when she came to faith in Christ. Susie became a good friend and a vibrant Christian, bringing her vitality to the work of Christ. When Susie Smith became confined to a wheelchair by multiple sclerosis, she still flashed that same sparkling smile, warmed even more by the love of Christ.

We have experienced substantial joys in professional ministry, but nothing is quite so fulfilling as the personal joy of seeing family friends come to faith. Our children feel as strongly about this as we do, and the times we have reminisced over our family's ministry have been particularly sweet. Together we have shared tears and laughter over a boy who was our children's childhood friend. Though he was a constant presence in our home, he never seemed to get the picture. But after he was married and difficulties came, he got the picture! His cross-country call telling us that he had come to Christ and had been baptized is a family highlight. One of Heather's little friends joyfully came to believe before she died of cystic fibrosis. Heather, then in grade school, wrote this remembrance:

> *Everyone who knew her*
> *loved her*
> *and they still do*
> *even though all that is left here*
> *is a memory.*

Another time we rejoiced at a phone call from the mother of a young man who worked with our son Kent, expressing her appreciation for Kent's influence in her boy's life. And Carey's junior-high buddy, despite his father's being a national spiritist leader, was marvelously converted and today is a godly father and spiritual leader. The very vacation home in which we began and finished this book belongs to our neighbors who became Christians through our family's witness.

So we are high on family ministry. And it is with a sense of celebration that we share something of what we have learned as a family.

THE FAMILY AS A VEHICLE TO MINISTRY

A young couple preparing for the mission field and recently engaged expressed concern. As the bride-to-be expressed it, "I want to have a family and children, but I also want to have a ministry." She voiced an increasingly common refrain among Christian women who imagine that unless they have a professional-style ministry outside the home, utilizing their education and talents, they don't have a ministry.

We believe this is an unfortunate delusion. Aside from the obvious objections (namely, that such thinking reveals a shriveled view of parenting, and the fact that good parenting requires every ounce of intelligence and creativity one can give), it also fails to recognize that family is at the very heart of authentic ministry and evangelism. As ministry professionals, we hold the firm conviction that family *is* ministry and that the most effective spread of the gospel occurs through family. We are also convinced that we were never more effective in evangelism than when we had children at home.

At the heart of the "family is ministry" equation is the fact that children naturally befriend the children of people with whom we rarely would have significant exchange. Children also naturally cross barriers that their parents find daunting, if not impossible, to bridge. We had an unforgettable experience when our boys became friends with the son of an Iraqi Jewish family who had recently fled Muslim persecution. None of the family had yet mastered English, but our son Kent's friendship paved the way for our families to host each other over memorable oriental and occidental meals — and also led to their son visiting our church. Children liberate us from the Christian insularity that segregates us from those who need Christ — an important element in missions and evangelism.

Another reason why family is ministry is that healthy Christian families are magnetic. Despite the prevalent objections of the sociological establishment, the nuclear family is most natural to human existence. The Holy Trinity itself is "family" (Father, Son, and Holy Spirit); those in Christ are "family" (brothers and sisters); and the original Genesis intent for humanity was family. Therefore, when Christian families are living under God's Word, people will find themselves drawn to them. Despite our many deficiencies, we found this to be repeatedly true over the years.

A further reason that Christian families are so often magnetic is that parenthood tends to open couples to spiritual realities. The miracle of birth often causes people to reflect on the eternal. The terrifying intensity of the love they feel for their children motivates other parents to consider their children's eternal destiny, even if they have never been con-cerned about their own. This is why pastors regularly get inquiries about baptism and confirmation from unbelieving parents, such as the mother who said, "I don't care what you do, Preacher, as long as you get some water on him!" Often the spiritual openness is inarticulate; parents just feel a need. Thus Christian families that radiate spiritual life often have wonderful opportunities to share the love of Christ.

In this connection Christians who truly love their neighbors' children will naturally have God-given opportunities to share their faith. On occa-sion we found that otherwise gruff, hard-hearted parents became surpris-ingly congenial, even open, because they knew we loved their children.

And, of course, children naturally witness, even when their parents are shy about it. Holly, who was so persistent in her witness to her kindergarten teacher, saw it come full circle when she took her own chil-dren to the park. Brian, a kindergartner, began to converse with another little boy atop the slide. Holly had sat down next to the boy's mother and exchanged a few pleasantries when Brian suddenly called to his mother, "Hey, Mom! Joey doesn't know Jesus!" It was hardly a presentation of the gospel, but young Brian was on the right track. He was asking the big questions.

Children are wonderfully open about their faith. We once overheard Carey talking to his grade-school friends about the wonders of heaven. It was during the era of the popular TV series *The Six Million Dollar Man,* and as Carey's voice rose with heavenly enthusiasm, he reached for the ultimate of metaphors: "It's . . . it's better than bionic!"

Believe it. Family *is* ministry.

THE DISCIPLINE OF FAMILY MINISTRY

Building a family ministry involves living out some joyous disciplines. They include the following:

Keep an Open House

From the start, we followed the advice of Howard Hendricks that we were "growing children, not grass." There would come a day when we would have a "grandparents' house" with light carpet and *objets d'art* within casual reach. But the child-raising years were the Tupperware years.

When our children were growing up, there were ten houses on our block, and six of the homes, including ours, had a pool. Although five of the six had children who were peers to ours, our pool was the only one to which all were regularly welcome.

On most afternoons and many evenings, June through August, our pool was busy — sometimes in shifts. Our summer memories are of hot days redolent with chlorine (busy pools require large daily doses), the sound of children playing and squabbling and calling "Mrs. Hughes," the daily diving contests — "That was a three, Rob!" "No way, Kent! It was at least a nine!" — and the picture window perpetually streaked by the splashes of the forbidden cannonballs.

Admittedly this was inconvenient and sometimes disruptive, and there were times when everyone was sent home. But the benefits far outweighed the inconveniences. At the top of the list was the fact that we knew where our children were — at least most of the time; so we had *some* control over the influences that crossed their lives. The Hughes family also gained a reputation for hospitality, and this in turn increased our influence. We got to know children and parents in a very comfortable way, which paid benefits over the years.

We cannot overemphasize how important an open house is — an extra place at the table for a neighbor's child, room for another body to be squeezed into the backseat to go to see Disney's newest film or go to the beach or go to *church*. It is not without significance that church leaders are to be "hospitable" (1 Tim. 3:2). An open house builds the body of Christ.

Resolve to Like Your Children's Friends

Barbara loves children — other people's children as well as her own. She has always looked little people in the eye and greeted them with a merry "Hello!" that says, "I think you're wonderful!" In this she is never insincere or patronizing, for she truly loves all children. Children sense that they are regarded as *people* and know that Barbara takes them seriously. Their parents have also sensed it and have liked and appreciated her for it.

There is a common-sense truism here: "In this cold, hard world, you like my children, and I'll like you! And maybe I'll even give some thought to what you stand for." We have also experienced this from the other side. We have appreciated and respected those men and women who have truly liked our children, and especially those who have given them some time.

Teenagers are no different. They like to be liked and *know* when they are. Kent Graham, one of Carey's friends, was an unusually large junior high kid with huge hands and feet — reminding us of a growing St. Bernard. Kent knew that Barbara loved him. And his response? Typically it was to stoop and hug her, saying, "Hi, little mamma" as he patted her on the back. In late years we saw Kent play quarterback for a series of professional football teams, and when we saw defensive linemen giving him a "squeeze," we thought of those hugs.

Cherish children, and you will have a ministry.

Pray for Other People's Children

There was a man who prayed, "Lord, bless me and my wife, my son John, and his wife. Us four, no more." Down the street a couple prayed, "Lord, bless us two, and that will do!" And around the corner lived a bachelor who intoned, "Lord, bless me; that's all I can see."

Hearts that have room only for their own "family," as it is conveniently defined, are shriveled hearts, shamefully out of sync with the pulse of the Master's heart. Common sense dictates that if we desire to have a family ministry, we must pray for those families with whom our lives intersect. Our personal prayer lists have such names on them. Some have been there for decades. And we will see some come to Christ, for God delights to answer such prayers.

Be a Source of Neighborhood Fun

We recall a year in which every Thursday, beginning six weeks before Christmas, Barbara invited the neighborhood children over to eat home-baked cookies and practice Christmas caroling. Our hope was to involve their parents as well. Barbara's practice sessions were not devoted to musical excellence, but simply teaching the children the words and charging them with enthusiasm. And sure enough, as Christmas approached, the enthusiasm peaked and spread to their moms and dads. Parents began to call and offer help. One mother volunteered her home for an after-caroling party. Others agreed to bring Christmas goodies.

When the evening came, we were especially excited because it was the coldest night of the year (in California that is the mid-thirties); so the children could really bundle up the way you are supposed to when you carol. Feeling like part of a Christmas card portrait, we sang throughout the neighborhood, escorted by an entourage of happy parents.

Later, at the brightly decorated home, we sang again, adults and all, and there Kent told the Christmas story. For some, it was the most religious thing they had done in years. They heard the gospel, and they liked it.

On another occasion, our family organized a "pet parade," in which each child decorated a wagon and paraded his or her pet. The "floats" bore cats, dogs, lizards, birds in cages, and hamsters. If we had had a video camera, the event would have qualified for *America's Funniest Home Videos*. Cats clawed dogs, animals bolted, wagons went awry — and everyone had a ball. The event moderated secular culture's stereotype of Christians being dull and joyless and further identified our Christian family as happy and life-affirming.

Common sense tells us that winsomeness is vital to a family ministry.

Be Kind to Your Neighbors

We recall an occasion when our missionary friends had been looking forward to furlough because their time on the field had been particularly stressful. The wife's anticipation was the greatest because for the first time in her life she was going to have her very own home. They had been able to save just enough to invest in a new townhouse-style apartment with a lovely patio.

Spirited and creative, she used her talent and what she could squeeze from her meager budget to make the patio the focus of her decoration. It was, in everyone's estimation, a remarkable success. And she began to enjoy her much-needed quiet and to relax.

Then new neighbors moved in. The kindest word to describe them was *coarse*. They played loud music day and night and constantly shouted obscenities at one another. The men urinated shamelessly on the front lawn in broad daylight. Not only were they foul and ignorant, but they seemed to have marginal mental capacity. Her peace evaporated. She could see no good in them at all.

During this unpleasant time, our friend had been praying that the Lord would make her more loving. But all she could feel was disgust and rejection. And it got worse, for one dark day she returned home from shopping to discover that her neighbor's children had climbed the wall, found a can of orange paint, and splashed it all over her beautiful patio — floors, walls, ceiling, furniture, everything.

She was distraught and furious. She attempted to pray, only to find herself bitterly weeping and crying out, "I hate them! I hate them! I can't love them!"

As her emotions receded, she knew that she must get her heart right, and again she began to pray. As she prayed, Colossians 3:14 came to mind: "And above all these put on love, which binds everything together in perfect harmony." "Lord, how am I to do this?" she responded. "It seems so false."

In an instant she understood: She must put it on like a coat. So that is exactly what she did. She imaginatively wrapped herself in the coat of God's love. Then she made a list of what she would do if she really loved them. She baked cookies and took them to the family. She offered to baby-sit the very children who had ruined her patio. And she invited the mother over for coffee.

Our dear friend had volitionally put on love, which manifested itself in profound kindness. And the love was real. In fact, she began to understand them, and she came to appreciate their pressures as she took the time to listen to her neighbor pour out her heart. During one of these visits she was able to share Christ, though the woman did not respond — at least at that time.

Then came the day when the neighbors abruptly had to move. And she wept.

Become Involved in the Community

Kent was once roped into coaching for the local youth soccer league (he can't claim that "ministry" was his reason for coaching). To his surprise, he stepped out onto the chancel for Sunday worship one morning to discover his entire team, the Awesome Aztecs, wearing their orange and black jerseys, sitting in the front row. Their parents (Hindus, Jews, Mormons, and others from various Christian traditions) sat behind them, beaming. It was their way of showing appreciation for the time Kent had taken for their sons.

More unbelievers heard the gospel that day than in any regular three months in our little church. Humanly speaking, it was all because Kent hadn't been able to bring himself to do the rational thing and say no to coaching. In retrospect, of course, it was all so logical: If you want to become a witness to people outside your church, you must be with them.

SUMMARY

The path to a life-changing family involves some remarkably joyful disciplines:

- Keep an open house.
- Like your children's friends.
- Pray for others' children.
- Be a source of neighborhood fun.
- Be kind to your neighbors.
- Become involved in the community.

There is not an ounce of hyperbole in our affirmation that though we have had remarkable joy in a "successful" public ministry, nothing has been as fulfilling as seeing family friends and neighbors come to Christ.

It is unfortunate when Christians separate family and ministry, because family, correctly understood, *is* ministry. Believe it. Live it to the glory of God.

FOOD FOR THOUGHT

Is "family ministry" (ministry by your family, working together) a dream or a reality (or at least a realistic possibility)? Can even young children be part of this? How?

Do you agree that family is ministry? Why or why not?

How do we know that family is close to the heart of God?

Do you agree that a Christian home should be open to other kids, neighbors, etc.? What risks could this carry? What benefits and opportunities?

In what ways can parents become involved in the community in order to minister to others? In what ways are you involved? In what other ways could you be involved or desire to be?

7

Discipline of Instilling Healthy Self-regard

The recipe box was beautiful, one of a kind. A sturdy grass-green cardboard box decked with hand-painted mushrooms, it was much too expensive for our budget, but Barbara won it at a baby shower, and it was *hers* — guilt-free! She liked it so much that it became the motivation for organizing a drawer full of recipes, which over the weeks she painstakingly recopied on three-by-five cards and carefully filed.

Finished with the project, she placed the box on the kitchen table, then stepped back and observed its luminous green glory. Satisfied, she went about her daily routine. Her day was soon happily interrupted by several friends, who "kidnapped" her for a birthday luncheon, leaving one of the older children to baby-sit. Two hours later Barbara light-heartedly walked back in the front door, announced, "I'm home," and glanced at the kitchen table where the box *had been*. Alarmed, she was just about to cry out, "Where's my recipe box?" when seven-year-old Kent approached with a pleased smile on his shy face. He was holding something behind his back, from which water was dripping onto the tile floor.

In a sinking instant Barbara knew that it was her beloved recipe box. Swallowing hard, she asked what he had behind his back. "A present for you," he proudly responded, presenting her with a soggy cardboard box sans mushrooms!

Kent had observed how much his mother liked the box, and he wanted to do something nice for her birthday. He had emptied the recipes in the curbside trash cans (and the trashman had come!), then washed the box in the bathtub, lined the box with tinfoil, and placed three treasures in the box: a prized black plastic alligator he had been perpetually carrying about, a tarnished nickel, and a photograph of himself. When Barbara looked at the photo, he said, "Mom, I know you like my face." Barbara wrapped her little guy in her arms and lavishly thanked him.

It was a very important moment because Kent's early learning disabilities had so devastated his self-esteem that he would not look others in the eye. Barbara had been repeatedly insisting that he look her in the eyes, telling him, "I like your face, Kent."

We still have the foil-lined box and its three treasures. In fact, it is a family heirloom, valued by all, not the least by Kent himself. That was not the end of his self-esteem problems, of course. But today Kent has a firm handshake and clear, cheerful, engaging eyes.

We were very aware of the importance of self-esteem, and we worked hard to develop it in our children. We are proponents of *biblically informed self-regard* when it is properly understood and applied. Indeed, the Scriptures encourage a proper self-regard. A proper self-regard is realistic, as the Bible itself declares: "For by the grace given to me I say to everyone among you not to think of himself more highly than he ought to think, but to think with sober judgment, each according to the measure of faith that God has assigned" (Rom. 12:3).

THE CULT OF SELF

In contrast to this biblical approach, the secular self-esteem movement and its religious counterparts, which have achieved the dubious distinction in modern American life of being both politically and religiously correct, are perceived as panaceas for all individual and societal ills.

At the heart of self-esteem's groupthink is the passionate belief that a positive self-regard is the solution for all social evils, public and personal. The comedian who played Pee Wee Herman, arrested for lewd behavior, was partly excused in the thinking of one religious scholar who declared, "Masturbation isn't the problem; it's a lack of self-esteem."[1]

The writer was simply repeating the popular philosophy that deviant behavior is evidence of a self-image deficiency. So entrenched is this thinking that citizens in Florida were recently warned to be on the lookout for a serial rapist described as a man in his thirties, of medium build, and having a "low self-esteem."

The belief that a positive self-esteem is a societal cure-all was given its most doctrinaire expression to date by the California State Task Force on Self-Esteem and Personal and Social Responsibility. Despite conflicting scientific evidence, the Task Force's report concluded:

> Self-esteem is the likeliest candidate for a *social vaccine* [emphasis in original], something that empowers us to live responsibly and that inoculates us against the lures of crime, violence, substance abuse, teen pregnancy, chronic welfare dependency and educational failure.[2]

The uncritical acceptance of this view has spawned a huge self-esteem industry evidenced by the advent of the High Self-Esteem Toys Corporation and the proliferation of self-esteem day-care centers where the word *bad* is never spoken and an awards ceremony is held every six weeks.[3] Thus according to the social planners, all one needs is an injection of self-esteem, and the way is clear to societal sainthood!

The religious version of the cult of self is the erroneous belief that self-love unlocks the Christian faith. As recorded in Matthew 22:37-40, Jesus said:

> *You shall love the Lord your God with all your heart and with all your soul and with all your mind. This is the great and first commandment. And a second is like it: You shall love your neighbor as yourself. On these two commandments depend all the Law and the Prophets.*

Proponents of the self-esteem movement interpret this to contain not two, but three commands: Love God, love your neighbor, and love yourself! The third, self-love, is taught to be the key to the others. "You can't love God or others unless you love yourself." Thus the modern Christian life is grounded on self-esteem rather than humility, in contrast to the practice in previous generations.

The Errors of the Self-Esteem Movement

So then, what are our major criticisms of the self-esteem movement? We will note two: it is *unbiblical*, and it is *self-absorbed*.

Unbiblical. The immediately apparent flaw is the unfounded assertion that Jesus' words command self-love. In reality, he gives only two commands — love God, and love others. Had Jesus meant a third commandment, he would have said, "and the third is. . . ." The command "Love your neighbor as yourself" simply presumes the universal fact that people naturally love themselves. "No one ever hated his own flesh, but nourishes and cherishes it" (Eph. 5:29). Jesus simply commands his followers to love their neighbors as much as they love themselves. Therefore, to read even the slightest idea that you are commanded to love yourself into Jesus' words "Love your neighbor as yourself" is to twist the Scripture.

The unbiblical nature of religious self-love ought to be apparent to us because self-love is the scriptural equivalent of sin, not virtue. Paul exhorts Timothy, "But understand this, that in the last days there will come times of difficulty. For people will be lovers of self . . . rather than lovers of God" (2 Tim. 3:1-2, 4). Love of self deflects love from God.

Christians must also remember that the first person to read the necessity of self-love into Jesus' words "Love your neighbor as yourself" was not a Christian, but the self-declared humanist psychologist Erich Fromm.[4]

Self-absorbed. Humanity has always gravitated toward sinful self-focus. But today many promote self-absorption as a virtue — which makes it even more beguiling to those already nursed on the propaganda of self. Shirley MacLaine's famous praise of self-centeredness has become the "primrose path" for multitudes:

> The most pleasurable journey you take is through yourself . . . the only sustaining love involvement is with yourself. . . . When you look back on your life and try to figure out where you've been and where you are going, when you look at your work, your love affairs, your marriages, your children, your pain, your happiness, when you examine all that closely, what you really find out is that the only person you really go to bed with is yourself. The only person you really dress is yourself. The only thing you

have is working to the consummation of your own identity. And that's what I've been trying to do all my life.[5]

Amid seductive siren songs like this, if we are to have any hope that we or our children will escape the gravitational pull of our culture's self-centeredness, we must critically reject all earthbound schemes of building self-esteem and assist our children toward a biblical self-regard. Ultimately, the destiny of their souls may rest upon our doing this, because *secularized self-esteem* promotes *self-deception* regarding one's spiritual needs, which can then lead to eternal *self-destruction*. So it is important that we bring a biblically informed discipline to this matter of self-esteem.

DISCIPLINES OF SELF-REGARD

Two disciplines are necessary for a healthy self-regard: *a proper self-focus* and *an overriding God-focus*.

A Proper Self-focus

An appropriate self-focus is at once both negative and positive. First, the Bible informs us that we are all radically sinful in the root of our beings. *Radical* comes from the Latin word *radix,* which means "root." All children, like their parents before them, are rooted in fallen Adam (see Rom. 5:12). The perfect, infallible portrait of every soul who has ever lived was painted by Paul in Romans 3:10-11: "None is righteous, no, not one; no one understands; no one seeks for God." Sin is so rooted in us that every part of the human personality is tainted. This, of course, doesn't mean that all people are as bad as they can be or that they don't do good things (see Luke 11:13). But it does mean that apart from God's grace and the God-ordained graces of human discipline, children will naturally gravitate to sin — quite apart from the tricks of the devil or their "corrupt" little friends.

This is definitely not the way the self-esteemers regard humanity in general and children in particular. Proponents of the self-esteem movement think that people are naturally good and that what they need most is wholesale affirmation, which will enable them to rise to their innate goodness. After all, "self-esteem is . . . a social vaccine." This is why, in some places today, parents who believe otherwise are considered dangerous reactionaries. But Christian parents must understand that their children need God's sanctifying grace in their lives. By nature they are sinners.

This doesn't mean, however, that the spiritually informed should have a morbid preoccupation with their wretchedness. Our two-year-old granddaughter Catherine gave us a start one morning when we heard her talking to herself, repeatedly lisping, "I'm a despicable person. . . . I'm a despicable person. . . ." *Gulp!* What had she been hearing, and where? We were relieved to find out that her mentor was the great theologian Donald Duck. Even her lisp was the same.

Here we must say that it is a grave mistake to repeatedly call your child a "bad boy" or "bad girl" when disciplining him or her. Instead, the bad actions should be pointed out: "You did a bad thing. . . ." or "You made a bad choice." Though it is true that they are innate sinners, "bad boy" is a declaration of character. The overuse of the epithet can have a prophetic, tragic effect, inducing in the child the grim resolve, "I'm bad, and so I will do bad things." Wise parents will learn to communicate to their children that they are sinful without assaulting their character or instilling despair.

The most important reason parents must help their children understand their sinfulness is that an understanding of one's condition is necessary for comprehending one's need for the radical work of Christ on the cross and for radical grace. As Charles Spurgeon so eloquently put it:

> *The first link between*
> *my soul and Christ is*
> *not my goodness*
> *but my badness;*
> *not my merit*
> *but my misery;*
> *not my standing*
> *but my falling.*

Similarly, the renowned Christian psychologist Paul Tournier has observed:

> Believers who are the most desperate about themselves are the
> ones who express most forcefully their confidence in grace. . . .
> Those who are the most pessimistic about man are the most opti-

mistic about God; those who are the most severe with themselves are the ones who have the most serene confidence in
divine forgiveness. . . . By degrees the awareness of our guilt and
of God's love increase side by side.[6]

There is great grace in the negative, and this is especially apparent
when we couple it with a positive self-focus, rooted in the fact that all
humanity is created in the image of God (see Gen. 1:27).

Consider this: Though one could travel one hundred times the
speed of light, past countless yellow-orange stars, to the edge of the
galaxy and swoop down to the fiery glow located a few hundred light
years below the plane of the Milky Way, though one could slow down
to examine the host of hot, young stars luminous among the gas and
dust, though one could observe, close-up, the proto-stars poised to burst
forth from their dusty cocoons, though one could witness a star's birth,
in all one's stellar journeys one would never see anything equal to the
birth and wonder of a human being. For a tiny baby girl or boy is the
apex of God's creation! But the greatest wonder of all is that the child is
created in the image of God, the *imago Dei*. The child once was not; now,
as a created soul, he or she is eternal. His or her soul will exist forever.
When the stars of the universe succumb to stellar destruction, that soul
shall still live.

Being created in the image of God further means that this soul has
a delicate moral sensibility that can ultimately conform to God. Being
made in his image means that each soul is a maker, a poet, a person who
can do good works when re-created in Christ Jesus. No angel can rival
the merest baby, for no angel is made in the image of God. This is where
biblical self-regard must begin. Indeed, all children are "fearfully and
wonderfully made" (Ps. 139:14).

Wonderful as this concept is, the self-regard of the regenerate child
of God extends even deeper, because a Christian is loved and accepted
by God and has a radically new status with God. He or she has been *ransomed* by Christ. Jesus declared that he came "to give his life as a ransom
for many" (Mark 10:45). Obviously Christians are of great value to their
Savior.

God's children are not only ransomed but *reconciled*. Our sin
estranged us, but "God was reconciling the world to himself, not count-

ing [our] trespasses against [us]" (2 Cor. 5:19). We were enemies of God, but now we can regard ourselves as friends of God — accepted.

In addition to being ransomed and reconciled, the child of God is also *justified* (see Rom. 5:1). The Greek verb translated *justified* carries the sense of "to count someone as righteous" or "to esteem someone as righteous." This status is a gift. As Alister McGrath has said, "Justification is thus about our status in the sight of God. It is the way we are viewed by the most significant of all others — God."[7] And since human self-esteem is conditioned by how we believe we are received by others, our justification is a major pillar in positive, biblical self-regard.

Lastly, the child of God is *saved* (see Acts 4:12; 13:26; Eph. 1:13; Heb. 1:14). The biblical word for salvation carries a dual meaning: "rescue" and "wholeness." Being rescued by God brings wholeness. Before Christ we were incomplete, and sin distorted the image of God in us. But salvation effected the restoration of God's image, the reconciling of our soul to God.

Putting it all together, we see that a child's proper self-regard comes from a dual focus that is at once *negative* and *positive*. A child must understand that he or she is a sinner whose entire person is tainted by sin and will therefore tend toward sin apart from God's grace. Sin comes naturally. But a child is also made in the image of God and is the apex of creation. Even more, if the child is a believer, the child is perfectly accepted by God — *ransomed, reconciled, justified,* and *saved*. Joanne McGrath and Alister McGrath, in *The Dilemma of Self-Esteem*,[8] demonstrate that the objective basis of self-esteem lies in the realities of ransom, reconciliation, salvation, and justification.

A Proper God-Focus

When we have instilled a proper self-focus in our children, we have taken a great stride toward proper biblical self-regard. But when that is coupled with a proper God-focus, it takes on full biblical dimensions.

Adoption. The fatherhood of God tells us not only that we bear the image of God as natural children, but that as believers we have been adopted as his children with all the rights that such a status implies. We were not only *created* by God but also *chosen* to be part of his family. One evidence of our being "family" is the inclination to call him "Dearest Father — Abba Father":

For you did not receive the spirit of slavery to fall back into fear, but you have received the Spirit of adoption as sons, by whom we cry, "Abba! Father!" The Spirit himself bears witness with our spirit that we are children of God.—Rom. 8:15-16

How elevating loving adoption is to one's self-regard.

Pedigree. People naturally tend to derive their self-esteem from pedigree. Children do this when they boast, "My daddy is stronger than yours!" Similar pride in heritage is seen in the length to which people go to preserve their ethnic traditions. But as believers we have ultimate family connections. As to earthly descent, if we are children of faith, then Abraham is our father. As to heavenly descent, we are born of Christ (John 3). "My Daddy is God!" Now that is the ultimate in pedigree!

Inheritance. Many others derive their significance from the inheritance that will be theirs. That is why people take note of surnames like DuPont and Rockefeller. But God's children have them all beat, for they are "fellow heirs with Christ" (Rom. 8:17). As we read in Ephesians 2:6-7,

[God] raised us up with him and seated us with him in the heavenly places in Christ Jesus, so that in the coming ages he might show the immeasurable riches of his grace in kindness toward us in Christ Jesus.

His children are heirs of the universe itself — and heaven beyond. Self-regard? We're sons of the King, and we must not forget it.

Paternal care. Lastly, there is the gentle, paternal care that fatherhood implies. God through his Son has suffered the ultimate for his children. Think, then, what this means in regard to his daily care.

> *He who hath heard thy cry*
> *Will never close His ear.*
> *He who hath marked thy faintest sigh*
> *Will not forget thy tear.*

Consider the implications of God's fatherhood: His children bear his image, his *likeness*; his children are *adopted*, for he deemed them of great value; his children have a *pedigree*, a name second to none; his children are *heirs* of the universe and heaven beyond; his children are objects of his *paternal care*. These truths together constitute the proper God-focus for the child of God and provide a solid foundation for self-regard.

DISCIPLINES OF SELF-REGARD

Bootstrap self-esteem programs will never do it. Making people feel good about themselves will not do it. The abolition of failing grades will not do it. Self-esteem toys will not do it. Awards ceremonies will not do it. Slogans such as "We applaud ourselves" will not do it. Calls to "celebrate yourself" will not do it. Cognitive therapy will not do it. Client-centered therapy will not do it.

The only solid source for healthy self-regard is the disciplined self-focus and God-focus that the Bible offers, which can be summarized this way:

> Self-focus:
> I am bad.
> I am wonderful.
> I am accepted.
> God-focus:
> I am fathered.

Today our own children have a healthy self-regard. But it isn't because we systematically catechized them in the subtleties of the subject — "Now, children, the first principle of the *imago Dei* is . . ." Rather, it is because the Bible has informed our understanding of who we and who our offspring are. We applied the biblical principles as part of a disciplined lifestyle and according to the flow of life.

First, I Am Bad

What did we do to instill in our children a proper understanding of their sinfulness?

First, we didn't shrink from labeling our children's actions "bad" or "good." We didn't cave in to the cultural pressure to avoid moral pronouncements. In other words, we called sin sin, though we were very careful not to repeatedly invoke the character-assaulting "bad boy" or "bad girl" epithet. The positive effect of calling sin what it is provided a clear-cut moral framework from which our children could see their need for God's grace.

Second, we didn't deny our children's individual responsibility for sin by blaming society (a common secular rationalization) or the devil (a common Christian gymnastic). In this area, children are sometimes wiser than we are — like the little girl who had a terrific fight with her brother. When her mother separated the two, she said, "Why did you let the devil put it in your heart to pull your brother's hair and kick him in the shins?" The little girl thought for a moment and said, "Well, maybe the devil put it into my head to pull my brother's hair, but kicking his shins was my own idea!" This naughty little girl had a very good sense of individual responsibility — no small blessing in this guilt-denying world.

Third, we disciplined our children when they did wrong. We weren't uptight or overly zealous about this, but we were consistent. This taught our children that sin has consequences. Again, this is a substantial grace in a self-justifying, no-fault culture.

Fourth, as our children grew older, we acquainted them with the scriptural realities of Romans 3 and other relevant texts regarding humankind's sinfulness. Children will generally understand more than parents think, and that understanding will further open them to grace.

Second, I Am Wonderful

There is substantive reason for God's children to understand that they are wondrous beings. They are made in God's own image and as such represent the zenith of his creation, being even more wondrous than angels. Each child is an endless being with moral sensibilities and a unique person capable of giving glory to God. Of course, we needed no encouragement to think our little darlings were wonderful! But understanding the scriptural realities enhanced our own practical application of their worth.

We tried to remind our children that they were unique creations from God's hand. We found that it is possible to celebrate this uniqueness from meals to bedtime prayers. Every child needs to be indoctrinated with the dizzying spiritual reality of his or her existence.

It is important to praise children whenever possible — not gratuitously but generously. It is a costly mistake to be stingy with praise, giving it only for extraordinary accomplishments, while wrongly imagining that "then my praise will really mean something." Honest praise does mean something. And children need a lot of it to develop a proper self-regard. It is especially important to praise character qualities and acts of generosity and kindness, as well as small accomplishments.

It is equally important to take care not to play favorites. Favoritism gives the lie to parental avowals that "each of our children is special." Untold numbers of people have struggled with self-regard to their dying day because of their parents' favoritism.

Along with this, we made conscious efforts to instill mutual esteem among our children. Name-calling and derogatory nicknames were forbidden. Our children were encouraged to celebrate each other's accomplishments so that they became each other's cheerleaders — a phenomenon that has joyfully remained into their adult years. A wise parent will understand that sibling regard is crucial to the development of good self-regard.

Another bit of wisdom essential to self-regard is to take great care to involve your children in activities at which they can realistically succeed if they try. Everyone knows that to insist that a two-year-old tie his shoes is unreasonable and personally damaging. Similarly, demanding that a nonmusical child become an accomplished pianist or that a nonathletic child make the basketball team can do immense harm to self-regard. Common sense tells us that we must progressively challenge our children within their growing capabilities. Wise parents will also involve their children in *some* activities that are noncompetitive, like fishing, stamp collecting, or baking, to name a few.

Third, I Am Accepted

When Barbara used to take the shy, diffident, sweet face of our boy in her hands and say, "Look at me — I like your face," she was affirming his worth, telling him that he was loved and accepted. Significantly, she was also shadowing the love and acceptance that God extends to his spiritual children.

Our acceptance of our children was unconditional. We did not make acceptance rest on a child's becoming or accomplishing something that we foisted on them. This is the error made by so many parents in today's success-driven culture as they consciously (or more often unconsciously) condition their children's acceptance on accomplishment. An A student is more accepted than a child who makes C's; the child who gets the lead in the school play senses greater acceptance than her brother who was stage manager; and in later life the child who "makes it big" is acknowledged over the one who "just gets along." This is neither God's way nor the way of wisdom. Our children must all be equally accepted.

In family relationships, a primary sign of acceptance is affection. We did not shrink back from lavishing affection on our children. Children cannot be hugged and kissed too much by *both* mom and dad. When our children were small, story time and bedtime sometimes looked like communal muggings! And our affection has remained over the years. Dad even gets an occasional kiss from his sons. Lay this to heart: Affection is the medium by which parents express acceptance.

Fourth, I Am Fathered

The importance of sensing the fatherhood of God cannot be overemphasized. Some say that the parallel fact of divine adoption is among the most healing of doctrines. Realizing this, we freely talked about God's fatherhood to our children. We attempted to act this out as we consciously imitated the divine model revealed in the Scriptures. And we embraced the divinely given impulse to pray "Dearest Father" in our prayers. Divine wisdom told us that a sense of our cosmic paternity had everything to do with proper self-regard.

The correct self-focus and God-focus supply can be instilled through the proper disciplines. They include four cardinal principles of self-regard: I am bad; I am wonderful; I am accepted; I am fathered. This is God's wisdom. It is the way to live, to parent, and to die.

FOOD FOR THOUGHT

Is self-esteem (self-regard) good or bad? What does Romans 12:3 say about this?

What are the errors of the secular self-esteem movement?

What does an awareness of personal sin have to do with a proper self-regard?

What does our being made in the image of God have to do with a proper self-regard?

Did you find the "I am bad. I am wonderful. I am accepted. I am fathered" outline helpful? How can you convey this to your children?

EVERYDAY LIVING

8

USING APPROPRIATE
DISCIPLINE

D r. Robert Coles, noted child psychiatrist, tells how, during his training at Children's Hospital in Boston, he discovered the importance of discipline in rearing children. He was assigned to a ten-year-old boy, described to him as having a "learning problem." The boy's behavior was rude, impatient, demanding, and without self-control during their sessions together. Dr. Coles tried reasoning with him, hoping to discover why he was behaving as he was, but each session only increased his own feelings of helplessness. Weeks passed in the same fashion — the boy having his way in the doctor's office and the doctor without a clue about how to help.

One snowy day when the boy arrived, he casually took off his boots and threw them, dripping slush, onto the doctor's chair. Dr. Coles recalls that he instinctively felt rage welling up inside him but at the same time heard an inner voice telling him that he must discover *why* the boy had acted as he had. Fighting to control himself, he walked to the chair, picked up the wet boots, put them in the hall outside his office, and slammed the door hard. When the boy responded that he wanted them inside the office, the doctor shouted, "Nothing doing!"

They were words the doctor had often heard his parents use during his own childhood when their patience had worn thin with his behavior. An astonishing thing happened: The boy sat down, looking as close to repentant as the doctor had ever seen him, and asked if there was something he could use to clean up the mess he had made. It was at that point that the doctor began to be able to help the boy. Dr. Coles writes:

> We are afraid to impose the obvious limits children need, in many cases because we think some psychological theory requires such an attitude. Ironically, if modern psychiatry has learned anything, it is a healthy respect for the darker side of our mental life and awareness of how important it is for all of us to have a sensible kind of authority over our impulses lest they rule us and, yes, ruin us, not to mention others we know.[1]

Dr. Coles had discovered something that the Bible taught long ago: We do no favor to children when we let them get away with bad behavior. In fact, Dr. Coles has become a persuasive advocate of judicious discipline.

Proper discipline needs to be governed by the right motive and purpose, it must be accepted as a parental duty, and it must be viewed as an expression of God-given authority.

THE BASICS OF THE DISCIPLINE OF CHILDREN

There are cultural reasons why discipline does not come easily to today's children and young people. The current generation of American children has been the recipient of the most massive self-esteem effort on record, going far beyond the legitimate affirmation of children that we encouraged earlier. In addition, today's children and young people are heirs of a cultural movement known as entitlement. A veteran teacher of our acquaintance claims to have seen in recent students a steady arc of increasing arrogance, overrating of abilities, inability to have work criticized, and condescension toward teachers.

Motive

The Scriptures clearly say that love is the Lord's motive when he disciplines us. Hebrews 12:5-6 is the classic expression of this truth:

> *My son, do not regard lightly the discipline of the Lord,*
> *nor be weary when reproved by him.*

For the Lord disciplines the one he loves,
and chastises every son whom he receives.

"The Lord disciplines the one he loves." Surely the same is true of our earthly family: Discipline demonstrates love.

Purpose

God uses the pain of discipline in our life because he wants the best for us. Hebrews 12:11 tells us, "For the moment all discipline seems painful rather than pleasant, but later it yields the peaceful fruit of righteousness to those who have been trained by it." Who among us doesn't desire such a harvest in the lives of our children? But without the pain there will be no harvest. In fact, the absence of discipline produces the very opposite. The undisciplined sons of Eli, for example, became *unrighteous* and *fractured* men. Their lives ended with them profaning the house of God, and their bodily appetites out of control (1 Sam. 2:12-17, 22-25). Excessive permissiveness and leniency, like Eli's, can result in spiritual disaster. We think also of the provocative statement in 1 Kings 1:6 regarding the rebellious Adonijah: "His father had never at any time displeased him by asking, 'Why have you done thus and so?'"

Duty

Discipline of children is not an option for Christian parents. It is a duty. Proverbs 22:6 instructs us to "train up a child in the way he should go," implying that there is a right way and a wrong way to train our offspring. It is our duty to train our children in the right way and to make it clear when that way has been violated. The responsibility for the choices our children ultimately make in following or rejecting Christ lies with them, but God will hold us responsible for disciplining them in the correct way.

Authority

Not only has God given us the responsibility of disciplining our children, but he's also given us the authority. We are astonished by the many parents we encounter who are impotent when it comes to administering discipline. They are powerless and appear unwilling to set clear limits or to demand proper behavior of their children. We believe this has happened because the conflicting advice of secular theorists has left parents so fearful of doing the wrong thing that they do nothing at all.

As biblically informed Christians, we must understand that children are *not* equal in authority with their parents. They are not little adults who must be reasoned with to obtain their consent for discipline. They are children! They need the instruction, training, guidance, protection, and discipline of parents if they are to grow to mature, secure adulthood. And God has given parents the authority to accomplish this; it lies in the structure of the family.

The classic passage in Ephesians 6 makes it clear that parents are to guide and children are to obey. Single parents in particular should draw courage from this truth. It doesn't take an expert to understand and implement this principle. It takes common sense and a little enlightened observation of what happens when parents abdicate their duty to discipline their children and set bounds.

Here is how the New England Puritan Cotton Mather imagined children addressing their parents on the Judgment Day for their neglect of parental discipline:

> You should have taught us the things of God, and did not; you should have restrained us from sin and corrected us, and you did not; you were the means of our original corruption and guiltiness, and yet you never showed any competent care that we might be delivered from it. . . . Woe unto us that we had such . . . careless parents.[2]

THE INVERTED TRIANGLE

Our approach to discipline is best explained by visualizing an inverted triangle. The narrow point at the base of the triangle represents the rigorous parental control we believe is necessary for young children. As the outward walls of the triangle ascend, they also widen, representing the proper loosening of parental control that yields to self-control. Finally, the walls reach the plateau, which symbolizes the goal: the *Spirit-controlled life.*

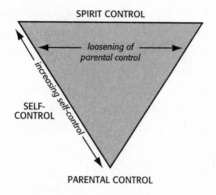

Parental Control

Children are not naturally self-controlled; they are dominated by their impulses, typically acting spontaneously with little thought. If young children are not disciplined by their parents — if they are not made to understand their boundaries and limits and are not well acquainted with what *no* means — then chaos will reign because the child will be in control.

Our observation is that most parents who lose control lose it when the children are very young. The first area that children can take control of is sleeping. Once babies have outgrown infancy, we must set their patterns for bedtime. After all, babies do not put themselves to bed — we do. But it doesn't take long for little ones to learn that their behavior can control you. If they do not want to go to bed when you want them to, they find that screaming and crying may upset you enough to make you change your mind. (Our comments here are for healthy children who have no established medical problems that might affect their sleep patterns; obviously, health issues should be taken into account.)

In the beginning, the resistance of small children to being put to bed seems to be a small matter. Infants sweetly smile and cuddle when you get them back up. And you reason, *What does it matter? A few more minutes, and* then *we'll put him to bed.* But the child's successful behavior begins to repeat itself over and over until it becomes a *very* big deal. And then regaining control becomes wrenchingly painful for both parent and child.

Another way children often gain early control is in eating. It happens just after infancy, when they begin to eat table food. Of course, all of us have certain foods that we sincerely do not like, and common sense tells us that we must respect children's taste to some degree. But when children control what they will and won't eat to the extent that their menu consists of two or three entrées and nothing else except junk food, you have a major problem. Through eating and sleeping patterns, babies often gain control and never relinquish it. (Common-sense tips regarding sleeping and eating are found in the appendix on pages 205-206.)

Nonnegotiable Early Directives

Maintaining control in the primary areas of sleeping and eating is essential to a good beginning in discipline. But no matter how well we begin, discipline will not succeed in the following years apart from three nonnegotiable essentials: respect, truthfulness, and prompt obedience.

Doesn't everybody know that children should be respectful toward parents, tell the truth, and do as they're told? Sadly, no. All three of these areas are subject to debate — as the heated discussions on the popular talk shows attest. If you want to have delightful children, kids that your friends enjoy being around, and ones that *you* enjoy too, pay attention to the following essential disciplines.

1. *Respect.* We read in Proverbs 30:17 that "the eye that mocks a father and scorns to obey a mother will be picked out by the ravens of the valley and eaten by the vultures." Of course this is a figurative statement, but it expresses a foundational principle of life — namely, that it will not go well for a disrespectful child. The commandment to "honor your father and mother" is linked with the promise of longer life for doing so (see Eph. 6:1-3). For this reason alone, parents who love their children ought to demand and expect respectful behavior.

Two areas are especially important: a respectful *demeanor* and respectful *words*. Respectful demeanor means that insolence, even a disrespectful glance, is not permissible. We've all seen the child who "obeys" but projects contempt through his expression. Truly, "if looks could kill," many parents would be dead. It may seem overbearing to our permissive culture, but for our children's sake we must not allow even the most subtle visual insolence. A mocking eye may portend a feast for the vultures.

Respectful words are music to parents' ears. Children must be taught early the difference between congenial exchange and disrespectful back talk. One might think this would be a problem only for older children. However, because little children are exposed to so much disrespectful slang today through the media, it is not uncommon to hear preschoolers referring to their parents as "losers" or sarcastically using expressions such as "give me a break." While such talk may appear cute coming from little people, it is actually establishing a frame of mind that puts parents on the level of peers. Our ego can certainly handle it, but again, God's Word and common sense tell us that this may spell an unpleasant future for the child who speaks in this way — because disrespect is taking subtle root.

2. *Truthfulness.* "You shall not lie," states the ninth commandment, thus providing reason enough to make truthfulness one of our nonnegotiables. But there is something more. We realized that our children would find truthfulness difficult because we live in a world that oozes with deceit. Doctrinaire news reporting masquerades as objectivity. The advertising industry is a form of institutionalized deceit. We live in a foggy netherworld of deception. Therefore, we had to consciously compensate by rigorous insistence upon telling the truth. Though speaking from the eighteenth century, the great Dr. Samuel Johnson gives this sage advice:

> Accustom your children constantly to this [the telling of the truth]; if a thing happened at one window, and they, when relating it, say that it happened at another, do not let it pass, but instantly check them; you do not know where deviation from truth will end. . . . It is more from carelessness about truth than from intentional lying, that there is so much falsehood in the world.[3]

Of course, we left plenty of space for playfully embellishing a story and for tall tales. But in the hierarchy of offenses in our family, our children would be less severely disciplined for some rather unacceptable behaviors than they would if they were caught lying. We *never* let our children off easy for lying.

Truth begets truth. Without it, our children will not have a chance in the spiritual battles that will come their way. Teach them to value truth. Proverbs 6:16-17 tells us that "the LORD hates . . . a lying tongue." God himself is "the God of truth" (Isaiah 65:16), and our children should be children of truth.

3. *Prompt obedience.* We insisted that our children understand that delayed obedience is disobedience. When they obey according to their own time schedule, they are in control. Immediate obedience is terribly important when children are very young; it can actually save their lives. If a child is running for the street and a car is swiftly approaching, he had better respond immediately to "Stop!" or disaster could follow.

It is also important when they are older — for reasons of character. Once when Barbara asked our junior high son to take out the trash, his response was, "Sure, Mom, later." She grabbed him by the shoulders, looked him straight in the eyes, and said, "No, I want you to take it out *now*."

"But why, Mom?" he wailed. "Why can't I take it out *later*?"

"I want you to take it out now, Son, because I'm raising a man, and men do things on time. Boys put things off till later."

With that, he straightened his shoulders and said, "Oh! OK, Mom." And out went the trash. Another brick in his character.

Obviously Barbara was appealing to our son's developing male ego. More importantly, she was appealing to his conscience. The implication of these words was that immature actions are often wrong, while maturity does the right thing. The conscience is a sort of warning system, a gift from God, that needs tending lest it become seared. Appeal to your child's conscience!

Our well-tried advice is to put everything you've got into building prompt obedience in the early years. Be strict; work hard; establish habits and patterns of obedience that will allow you to begin to loosen the control you have over your children's behavior as they approach adolescence.

Affirming Self-control

As progress is made upward on the inverted triangle, the walls widen, depicting a diminishing of parental control. If you have done your job in the early years, deep channels of self-control have begun to form in your child's will. Obedience and respect to parents will have become habitual, and the results will affect other areas where respect is essential.

Now is the time to begin to let go. Trust your child. Give him (or her) some space. He will make mistakes. And when he does, he will learn from the consequences, just as one of our sons did when he was twelve years old. Unfortunately, he had obtained a large supply of firecrackers. Although there was an ordinance against the use of firecrackers in our city, they were nonetheless the rage among preadolescents. Our boy discovered that he could make some easy money by becoming the neighborhood source.

Kent spoke to him several times, reminding him that not only was this not a good idea, but it was against the law. His response was always the same: "Oh, Dad, everyone's doing it." We wanted very much for *him* to make the right choice in this matter. We decided to wait and watch and pray.

A week later Barbara was busy preparing dinner when the telephone rang. The trembling voice on the other end of the line said, "Mom, I'm at the jail."

An hour earlier, two young friends had come by to see Carey. The three boys left together on their bicycles, headed for a field where they proceeded (unknown to us) to have a "war" — lighting firecrackers and launching bottle rockets. An annoyed neighbor called the police. The villains were caught red-handed.

The police officers made the boys ride their bikes directly in front of the squad car all the way to the police station (complete with flashing lights) while one of the policemen gave them directions through a bullhorn. "Turn right at the next corner. Slow down as you approach West Street, and turn left." By the time they arrived at headquarters, the boys were humiliated and terrified. That evening Kent brought home a very humble young man who immediately, without our saying a word, destroyed his entire cache of firecrackers.

As our children gained increased freedom, they made mistakes. But as we look back, we realize that their mistakes often made them tender to their need for the guidance of their heavenly Father. We also know that, along with their failings, God used our own mistakes to bring about his will in their lives. We sometimes did the wrong thing in our zeal to please God, but God is gracious with the failings of his children.

And so we confidently affirm that the right way to approach discipline is to begin with tight control in the early years and then loosen up as the children become older, rather than attempt to rein in children who have not known control for years.

Although it is a serious mistake to fail to gain control of your children in the early years, we believe it is equally ineffective and injurious not to let go at the proper time. If you want your sons and daughters to achieve the maturity of a life given over to the control of God, you must trust God and relinquish control to them. It is a spiritual axiom: Your children cannot give to God what they do not own.

Significantly, it was only a couple of years later that our son, whom we allowed to suffer the consequences of his illicit firecrackers, experienced a dramatic commitment of his life to God. While a Christian buddy was spending the night, they began to discuss spiritual matters. Carey fell under deep conviction of sin. Well past midnight, he stood trembling at our door saying, "Mom and Dad, you've got to pray for me. I want to give my whole life to God." In a momentous instant he stood atop the plane of the triangle. Of course, during his teenage years Carey fluctuated in his submission to God's control. But this signaled the beginning of his arrival.

God's Control

We knew that one day our children would grow up and leave home. That day came for all our children. Now our role as disciplinarians in the lives of our sons and daughters has ended. But their need of discipline has not. As parents, we have been replaced by two disciplines in the lives of our children — self-discipline and the discipline of God.

Barbara was humbled and caught short by these qualities in our married daughter Holly as the two of them stood at a customer service counter. It was a week before Holly's in-laws were to arrive for Christmas, and the wallpaper she had ordered three months earlier had not arrived — entirely due to the store's inefficiency.

Barbara was disappointed for Holly, and she was livid. She told Holly that if there was no satisfaction, she was going to give the clerk a piece of her mind. Holly stopped her in midsentence. "Mom, let's be different," she said. "Let's act like Christians." Our daughter was under God's control, and she was now teaching her mother.

Godly discipline in children leads to self-discipline and a dependence upon the guidance and discipline of God. One of the greatest gifts we can give our sons and daughters is the gift of discipline, which results in a life of righteousness and peace. (Tips regarding discipline are found in the appendix on pages 205-209.)

FOOD FOR THOUGHT

What does it mean to discipline children? Why is this so important?

"Parental control—self-control—Spirit control." Did you find this outline helpful? Which part is the most difficult for you? For your children?

Why is it important for children to respect their parents? What does Ephesians 6:1-3 say about this?

"Delayed obedience is disobedience." Do you agree? Why is it so hard to insist on prompt obedience, and so easy to let things slide? What are the consequences of each?

Which is more difficult—to have proper control of your children or to let them go when the proper time comes? Why?

9

Discipline of
Teaching Good Manners

≈

In the smogless Southern California of the 1950s, avocado orchards were nearly as abundant as orange groves. Avocados were almost as common a fare for dinner as orange juice was for breakfast. But that was true only to those living near the orchards, for avocados had not yet become the popular delicacy they are today.

A friend of ours vividly recalls her father bringing home a business associate from the East Coast for dinner one time when she was a child. The meal began with a first course of avocados sliced in half, the seed removed and the tender green flesh sprinkled with apple cider vinegar and salt and pepper. The halved avocados were served in their shell (a thick, green, bitter skin) and were to be eaten with a spoon, scooping out the fruit as if the shell were a bowl. The guest, unfamiliar with avocados, cut the avocado with his knife and fork and ate each bite, shell and all! The children, stunned by their guest's behavior, were even more taken aback when they saw their father follow his guest's example, eating his entire avocado in like manner. Having been well trained and reminded before dinner to "mind their manners," the children followed their father's example, choking down the inedible fare. What they recall today, however, is not the bitter taste but the sweetness of their father's remarkable concern for his guest. They learned the essence of good manners that evening: *respect for the feelings and needs of others.* Their father was willing to suffer a little unpleasantness rather than expose his guest's ignorance and possibly embarrass him.

TWO COMMON MISUNDERSTANDINGS

Children need to be taught the purpose of good manners, for if they do not understand the purpose, they will dismiss basic courtesies as unnecessary. Judith Martin, a.k.a. "Miss Manners," writes in her essay "Common Courtesy" that "all of us are born rude." She convincingly makes the point that it is the do-nothing school of childrearing that allows rude infants to develop into little savages.

Children are rude because they are so naturally egocentric. It's *their* needs, *their* comforts, *their* feelings that they demand be met — usually at the expense of weary parents. Of course, self-centeredness is natural, expected behavior in infancy and tolerable in toddlers, but it becomes downright unbearable in school-age children. Proper manners can be a most effective tool in teaching children that they are not the center of the universe. And as the realization grows, they will be well on their way to becoming civilized rather than savage.

Sadly, good manners have been minimized by many of today's adults. They wrongly imagine manners to be the snooty mastering of etiquette in order to establish one's superiority, so that one can look down at others and sneer, "Those people simply don't know how to behave." Nothing could be further from the truth. Manners are about respect and thus are rooted in the Christian ethic modeled by Christ — *my life for your life*. Self-sacrifice, therefore, is at the heart of manners. The apostle Paul held up the example of Christ as the rationale for being considerate to others when he told the Philippians, "Each of you should look not only to your own interests, but also to the interests of others. Your attitude should be the same as that of Christ Jesus" (2:4-5, NIV).

The Scriptures are clear about the ethic behind courtesy, but there are dedicated Christians who are ill-mannered. This was memorably impressed upon Kent the first day he left his new push-button umbrella hanging in the seminary reception area during class. When he returned, it was gone — "borrowed" by another student, who returned it bent and broken with a blasé, "Sorry." Kent ceremoniously dropped the mangled remains in a wastebasket and went to class. But unknown to him, another student saw what happened, retrieved the wretched thing, and took it to his workshop. That night the umbrella was hanging on the doorknob when Kent returned home. What a contrast the two preachers-to-be provided: The first was woefully ill-mannered; the second looked "to the interests of others." Significantly, the second man came from an outstanding Christian home where his parents modeled *my life for your life*.

TRAINING CHILDREN TO BE GRACIOUS

We consciously attempted to train our children to become gracious, well-mannered adults. Manners are not a wooden list of rules regarding the use of the right fork or word or posture. Rather, courtesy is flexible and subject to the needs and feelings of the people involved.

We found four common-sense elements helpful for disciplining our children in good manners.

1. *Teach your children that they are not the center of the universe; God is.* Everything they have, even life itself, is a gift from God. The Scriptures command all God's children to be grateful people who perpetually give thanks (1 Thess. 5:18; Phil. 4:6; Rom. 1:21). Self-pity and egocentricity are telltale signs of a self-centered, grouchy heart. Manners move us from self.

2. *Help your children discover that courtesy brings joy.* We can find genuine pleasure in helping those in need, whether it's an elderly woman needing assistance to cross the street or the person seated across the dinner table whose glass needs filling.

3. *Set the example.* Be gracious yourself. Let your example include being courteous to your own children when correcting their manners. Don't embarrass them.

4. *Understand that teaching ordinary, everyday etiquette will take disciplined work on your part.*

MIND YOUR MANNERS

The place to begin is with speech, because our choice of words reveals a great deal about us and our regard for others. An introduction can show either deference or disrespect. The purpose behind the rule regarding who is first presented to whom is simply to convey respect to an older person or a woman. Thus a younger person is always presented to an elder, and a man is always presented to a woman. Some may consider this old-fashioned, but it is a tried-and-true way to demonstrate and develop respect. Besides, when children learn the principle, they will be more at ease with new situations.

Introductions

Here are rules regarding introductions:

1. Always voice the older person's name before the younger: "Grandmother, I'd like you to meet Tommy Jones," or, "Mr. Pollard, this is Suzy Smith."

2. Always voice the woman's name before the man's: "Catherine Brown, may I introduce Chuck Brown," or, "Jessica, this is Tom Hinks."

If you forget the name of a person when introducing someone, simply say, "I'm sorry, I've forgotten your name."

Young children can easily be taught how to respond when their parents introduce them to new people. They should be taught to simply stand, look the person in the eyes, and respond with something like "Nice to meet you." As children grow older and are capable of learning the priorities of introduction, they can be taught in simple form: "Mom, this is Suzy. She's in my class at school." All they need to remember is to say "Mom" or "Dad" first.

Boys should understand that when they are introduced to other males, they should smile and extend their hand, firmly shaking hands while greeting the other with "Hi" or "Nice to meet you" or some other friendly variation. Boys should never shake the hand of a girl or woman unless she extends it to him.

Courteous Words

Children can learn the elements of courtesy when they are learning to speak, and some of their most-used words can become "please" and "thank you." The method of instilling this habit is so simple. Never respond to a screaming demand, say, for a cookie. Teach children that "cookie, please" is the way to get positive consideration. As children's mastery of words develops, the request should become a full sentence: "Mother, may I please have a cookie?"

"Excuse me" or "pardon me" is within the realm of a preschooler's vocabulary. Kent once took our young grandson fishing at a friend's pond. When the owner came out for a chat, young Brian pleased his grandfather when he tapped Mr. Morgan's hand and said, "Pardon me, Mr. Morgan, but I just wanted to thank you for letting us fish in your pond." Courteous children are nice to be around.

The Muppet Guide to Magnificent Manners neatly lists some very helpful tips for children learning to converse:

1. Try not to interrupt. If you must, say, "Excuse me for interrupting, but . . ."
2. Don't brag or exaggerate.
3. Don't pretend to know more than you do.
4. When someone compliments you, say "Thank you." Don't belittle the other person ("What, this old thing?") or get a swelled head ("Yeah, I know I'm great.").
5. Don't finish other people's sentences for them.
6. If you give an opinion, state it as such, not as fact.
7. If you disagree with someone else's opinion, don't say "You're wrong" or "You're crazy." Say something like "Do you think so? I don't see it like that."[1]

Here's our own list that emerged in our childrearing years:

1. Don't be a tattletale.
2. If you receive a gift you don't like, do your best not to show disappointment. And say something nice like "Thank you for remembering my birthday."
3. Don't gossip. If you do, you won't be a trustworthy friend, and you will displease God (Prov. 11:11-12; 18:13).
4. Don't whisper secrets in front of other people. The person left out will get hurt feelings.
5. Cheerfully greet the members of your family in the morning.
6. Always answer when you're spoken to — and do so respectfully.
7. When you haven't heard someone clearly, don't grimace in irritation, but kindly say, "Excuse me?"
8. Always address adults as Mr. or Mrs. or Miss, never by their first names. If they are particularly close family friends, your par-

ents may want you to call them "Aunt" or "Uncle." This shows respect. In the Southern states children use the friendly but respectful "Miss Suzy" or "Miss Martha" when speaking to adult acquaintances. The important thing here is developing a respect for authority, a quality sadly lacking in our country today.

Table Manners

We've spoken several times in this book about mealtime because it is so important. Edith Schaeffer has said that "Relaxation, communication and a measure of beauty and pleasure should be part of even the shortest of meal breaks."[2] We agree. Table etiquette is a vital part of making the experience pleasurable. The utensils are placed on the table for the convenience of the diners, even though one may think that only a fork is essential. A napkin is not "hoity-toity"; it is indispensable. And chewing with your mouth closed helps those eating with you maintain their appetite!

Meal planning and preparation should be a family affair. While someone is cooking the food, someone else should help set the table, and another fetch some extra chairs. Every member of the family should know and practice these basic skills and help be a part of making the pleasure.

Setting the Table

Don't make the mistake of thinking that the only time to set a nice table is when company is coming. While the fine china and lace tablecloth may be reserved for those times, the table should be inviting every day. Accumulate an adequate supply of place mats, tablecloths, and napkins, and keep them washed and ironed. Children can learn to iron by pressing napkins (though today most are permanent-press).

Teach your children how to set a table. Don't imagine that they will learn because you set it properly. We have known college students who did not know on which side of the plate to place the fork. So teach your children, and involve them in doing it regularly.

The table should be set as follows: The fork is placed to the left of the plate. The knife goes on the right of the plate, with the cutting edge facing the plate, and the spoon is placed directly to the right of the knife. If a soup spoon will be needed, it is placed to the right of the teaspoon, and a salad fork is located at the left of the dinner fork. The glass is placed just above the point of the knife. The bread plate or salad plate (or both if needed) is placed directly above the forks and to the left. The napkin may be placed to the left of the forks or in the middle of the dinner plate.

Taking the time to teach your children how to set a table is time well spent. They will thank you someday.

Setting the Scene

Once the table is set, be sure to add a centerpiece: flowers, fresh fruit, even a loaf of fresh baked bread and sometimes candles. The implicit message reflects the very heart of manners — "you are special." Finally, collect some nice dinner music. Play what your family prefers, but keep it low enough so as not to interfere with conversation.

We know some of you readers are thinking, *This will never happen!* Let us put you at ease. We don't believe that real people live like this *every* day. We admit that it was *rarely* idyllic with our family. But we are convinced that every family can work at it so that generally meals become times of affirmation and joy.

Dinner Is Served

Dinnertime with children is a most natural time for training. You must keep this and the big picture in view as you attempt to instill table manners. It takes years for good manners to become second nature; so be long-suffering and kind. A sense of humor is indispensable! Otherwise, dinnertime can be torture for children.

Here is our common-sense list of do's and don't's to assist you as you begin to train your children regarding the table:

1. Come to the table with hands and face washed.
2. Give thanks to God.
3. Place your napkin in your lap.
4. Wait until everyone is served and the hostess begins to eat before you begin.
5. Don't put your elbows on the table while eating or encircle your plate with your arms resting on the table.
6. Never say anything negative about the food.

7. When the food is passed, serve yourself small to medium portions.

8. Don't talk with food in your mouth.

9. Don't reach in front of another person for food. Simply ask, "Please pass the spinach."

10. Don't blow on your food if it is too hot; just wait till it cools down.

11. Learn to hold a knife and fork properly.

12. When you have finished eating, place your knife and fork atop the plate side by side.

13. Fold your napkin, and put it on the table.

14. Offer to help your mother clear the table.

15. Ask to be excused.

Mealtime Conversation

We have given advice on mealtime conversation in Chapter 3. Here are some additional tips to help your children learn how to participate in conversation with both family and guests.

1. Listen. When you are at the table, be *fully* there. You can't contribute to a conversation you haven't been listening to.

2. Learn to ask questions. Don't wait for someone to direct the conversation toward you.

3. Don't talk while chewing.

4. Has a family member had a bad day? Give a word of encouragement.

5. Don't "hold court" or hog the conversation.

6. Draw out the quiet person.

7. If conversation is lagging, bring up a new topic by making a general statement such as "Our youth group is going camping this weekend."

8. Don't interrupt.

9. Thank the cook!

BEING A GOOD HOUSEGUEST

The training you've given your children always shows best in someone else's home, when you're not present. When your children are on their own, suddenly manners become important! *What was it Mom said about my elbows on the table? Now wait till the hostess begins. Whoops! I'm chewing with my mouth open.*

Our children also appreciate having been taught these travel tips:

1. Take along a small gift and card, which you can sign with thanks and place in your room when you leave.

2. Use only the towels that have been given for your use.

3. Never leave the towels on the floor — hang them up.

4. Don't use the phone without asking, and *never* make long-distance calls (unless you're using a phone card you brought with you, so you're paying for the call).

5. Stay out of drawers, closets, and medicine chests unless you have permission to use them.

6. Bring your own toiletries.

7. Express gratitude for any food served to you.

8. Keep your dirty laundry out of sight.

9. Always wipe the basin and tub after use.

10. Make your bed every day.

11. Be very careful with your host's possessions.

12. Be as helpful as you can — clearing the table, drying dishes, etc.

13. *Never complain!*

14. Eat what is served to you unless you have some medical reason why you mustn't.

15. When you leave, remove the sheets from the bed, put them in the pillowcase, and leave the tidy bundle at the foot of the bed. Make up the bed without sheets.

16. *Flush the toilet!*

17. Don't wear out your welcome and risk taking advantage of your host's hospitality.

SOME FINAL TIPS

Finally, the following tips cover a variety of situations that your children will undoubtedly face in their growing years. (If your sons seem oblivious to the need for these tips, just tell them that someday they will need to make a favorable impression on their girlfriends' parents.)

If you are looking for more detailed assistance, we recommend that you visit the children's section of your local library and check out some of the numerous books on etiquette. You will be amazed at all the helps that are available to you and that your taxes have already paid for!

1. Knock before you enter a room if the door is closed.

2. If you chew gum in public, do it discreetly and with your mouth closed.

3. Return everything you borrow in the same condition as when you received it, *or better.*

4. If you lose or break something you have borrowed, even from a relative, replace it.

5. Cover your mouth when you sneeze or cough.

6. Teach your sons to show deference to the opposite sex and the elderly. Encourage them to offer to help you (the mother), or any woman, bring in the groceries or packages. Instruct them to unhesitatingly offer their seat to a woman or someone in need in a crowded public place. When walking with a female, boys should walk on the side closest to the street. They should help women and girls with their chair at the table and should open doors for them as well. Although a few women may think such actions are insulting or condescending, we have found that most women appreciate the courtesy.

7. Return telephone calls.

8. Promptly pay back any money you borrow — even a quarter.

9. Be respectful of national flags.

10. Be patient with service people who may find it difficult or confusing counting change or taking your order.

11. Teach your children how to behave with the handicapped. Discreetly explain why they may be different, but teach your children they are just like them, and certainly equals. Explain why most public places have wheelchair ramps and bathroom facilities designed to help the disabled. Instruct your children not to speak in a louder tone of voice to a handicapped person unless the person suggests it, and forbid them to stare. Teach them to treat the handicapped like everyone else, as naturally as possible. Above all, encourage your children not to shy away from conversation with handicapped people.

Manners *do not* make the man or woman. The radical reorientation that says "my life for your life" can only come from the regenerating work of Christ, who instills his life and ethic in us. Nevertheless, manners teach the need for and complement the character that Christ's life gives. Lives that say "my life for yours" are channels of God's grace to a needy world.

FOOD FOR THOUGHT

Why are good manners so important? How do they relate to a "my life for your life" mind-set?

How can we teach our children to be courteous?

Is insisting on table etiquette really important, or is this just majoring on minors? Explain.

Why is it valuable to teach our children how to engage in mealtime conversation?

What are the core values in teaching our children how to be good guests in other people's homes?

10

Discipline of
Fostering Lifelong
Enrichments

Sometimes a killer fog seeps into Christians and manifests itself in a gray, cheerless hostility to the excellencies of the world. We felt it particularly on one awkward occasion as we, along with some acquaintances, were marveling at the magnificent soprano Sarah Brightman's rendition of the Puccini aria *Chi Il Bel Sogno Di Doretta*. The moment of awed silence at the end was broken by one of our group saying with measured coolness, "I think that if you could hear the angels in heaven, you wouldn't be so impressed."

We could feel the wallpaper fade.

Perhaps when we ultimately do hear the angels around God's throne sing "Worthy is the Lamb," we *will* forget all earthly arias. And perhaps when we see Jesus face-to-face, our memories of sunsets and stars will grow dark. Perhaps. But we sincerely doubt it, because the rest of the song sung by the angelic host is this:

> *You are worthy, our Lord and God,*
> *to receive glory and honor and power,*
> *for you created all things,*
> *and by your will they existed and were created.* — Rev. 4:11

This song of worship invites our celebration, as does the whole of Scripture itself, which began with God repeatedly pronouncing creation to be "good." We believe that it is proper, even demanded, for God's people to rejoice in the excellencies of the world, whether they be those of a marvelous coloratura soprano or a giraffe, a whale, or a bird.

Christianity does not bring negation to life but affirms and enriches it. Jesus said, "I came that they may have life and have it abundantly" (John 10:10). And the Scriptures command that we live our life affirmatively to God's glory: "So, whether you eat or drink, or whatever you do, do all to the glory of God" (1 Cor. 10:31).

The purpose of this chapter is to provide some disciplines for enriching life in general — and especially the lives of children. We do not claim that children should necessarily share exactly the same cultural tastes as their parents, though respect for good culture remains a goal. Rather, our purpose is to bring a sense of wonder to all of life; to instill an attitude of gratefulness to God, the giver of all things; to increase the capacity to enjoy life to the fullest; to turn the soul upward in worship; and to turn it outward to serve. Borrowing from St. Irenaeus, we believe that one of the glories of God is seen when his children are fully alive!

READING

The time-honored road to enrichment is through books. Paul the apostle revealed his own fondness for them when he urged Timothy to come quickly and to remember to bring his coat, books, and parchments (2 Tim. 4:9-13).

Apart from the apostolic example, there are sound reasons to read. Disciplined reading exercises the mind. The mind responds very much like a muscle. Disuse atrophies it; exercise builds it up. Reading fills the mind, making us more interesting and more able to enjoy life. It also fires the imagination, enlarging our dreams and personal vision.

If, then, you desire that your children be enriched through reading, some personal disciplines are required. The first is be a reader yourself. If you are not a swimmer, you will not be a good swimming teacher. Your children will need to learn somewhere else. This principle applies to all areas of life. Studies have repeatedly shown that few children of nonreaders become readers.

Perhaps you used to read, but the busyness of family has stifled the habit. Don't give in! There is far more than your mind at stake.

One of the best parental disciplines is to read daily, with enthusiasm, to your young children. Mother and father should share the responsibility; otherwise the children may imagine it is a gender trait — "Reading is for girls!" Also read to your older children. On one rainy beach vacation, Kent read H. Ryder Haggard's *King Solomon's Mines* to our teenage sons and nephew. They couldn't get enough — they actually begged the poor man, "Dad, don't stop!" "Yeah, Uncle Kent, please!" Later that week the weather improved, but Haggard's classic remained the high point of the vacation. Michael Crichton's *Jurassic Park* is another page-turner; it's far more enthralling than the movie. Children of any age like to hear a story read. How our adult children still love it when at the holidays Kent reads aloud Truman Capote's *A Christmas Memory*.

Utilize your local public library. Our town has a population of only about sixty thousand, but it boasts a remarkable city library containing 330,000 volumes, with reference librarians who "live" to assist readers. Get to know your reference librarians. You'll be doing them and yourself a favor.

In addition to the vast variety of reading materials, children may check out audiotapes that include a book so they can see the stories as well as hear them. Many libraries also offer graded story times for toddlers, preschoolers, and kindergartners. In the summer there are also age-specific reading clubs.

Our library's resources (over eight thousand audiotape books and CDs) make possible many delightful "reading" options for virtually no cost. One of our friends listens to about forty books a year while traveling to and from work. Recently the two of us "read" Peter Mayle's delightful *A Year in Provence* as we chuckled our way home from Wisconsin. Many families shorten long trips with audio books that the whole family enjoys, like J. R. R. Tolkien's *The Lord of the Rings* trilogy.

Another helpful way to enhance reading is to have good books in the home. The appendix on page 211 contains a suggested reading list for children. Advice on adult books can be culled from reading the book review sections of Christian periodicals and reading books on books. (Kent's book *Disciplines of a Godly Man* has an appendix that lists the favorite books of thirty-four Christian leaders.) We also find the Sunday book review section of a great city newspaper a must. Read it regularly, and you will know what to avoid as well as what to buy. Even better, subscribe to *The New York Times Book Review*.

Lastly, we recommend visiting new and used bookstores. The big new stores have worked hard to create an inviting ambiance for adults and children so that they are fun places. Visits to good used bookstores with their museumlike atmosphere can breed youthful bibliophiles, like our boys. They were not always avid readers ("Mom, I'd rather do it than read about it"). But their interest was piqued during a brief stint in England. Carey began to collect C. S. Lewis, and Kent, Ryder Haggard. They both now possess some fine first editions and treasured memories of their finds. They also became enchanted by used bookstores — so much so that as teenagers they sat spellbound while watching *84 Charing Cross Road,* a very slow movie about correspondence between a New Yorker and a London bookseller. By the way, Helene Hanff's book by that title is far more enthralling than the movie. Reading is the ancient path to enrichment. Learn to walk it.

THE ARTS

When theologians speak about humans being created in the image of God, they don't mean that we have the physical form of God, but rather that we reflect some of his characteristics. We can love and think and feel emotion, and we also have the capacity to create. Animals cannot make works of art. Moreover, it is impossible to find people anywhere, in any culture, who do not create. Even if we determined to escape art, we could not.

Art is enriching because its primal impulse comes from God's image in us. At its best, it reflects God's image. Art also enriches because through it we are put in contact with the creative hearts of others from the ages. Of course, art has a tremendous power to debase as well as to enrich. The artistic impulse devoted to evil is profoundly corrupting, but when given to God it is profoundly elevating. That is why we parents need to be intentional regarding our children and the arts.

Music

Music is a vast source of personal enrichment. We recommend that families maintain a selection of good recorded music on tapes or CDs. This is especially important if you have decided (wisely, we think) to restrict television watching. In fact, if you have limited TV, some extravagance may be in order if your budget allows. Also remember that your library has hundreds of recordings that you can borrow.

As to selection, we must strongly emphasize that you *not* limit your collection to so-called "sacred music." Certainly you ought to have a selection of hymns and spiritual songs, but to play only this music is a mistake. In our opinion, much contemporary Christian music is written in an imitative style, and the lyrics are not as powerful or meaningful as they should be. More importantly, beautiful music brings glory to God apart from Christian lyrics. Christians are not relativists. Christians believe in objective truth and objective beauty. Some music is objectively beautiful and, as such, brings glory to God regardless of whether the composer was a Christian or not. Case in point: Mozart's piano sonatas.

Music does not have to be either sacred or objectively beautiful to be good — it is healthy for the family as long as the lyrics are acceptable. Songs that wholesomely extol romantic love, tell a story, celebrate everyday commonplaces, indulge in nostalgia, offer social critique — to cite some common themes — are not objectionable. Neither are specific musical styles. Folk, ethnic, country, jazz, even a rock album or two can be good listening. Our advice is to have your home selection weighted with the objectively beautiful classics (Mozart, Bach, Beethoven, Mendelssohn, Handel, Vivaldi) and play them often so that your home is full of beautiful music. Beyond that, be informed and eclectic in your choices.

Be sure to take your children to an occasional concert — when you know that the orchestra will be playing a famous piece with broad appeal so that your children will enjoy the evening.

Music lessons are, of course, enriching for children who have an aptitude for music. But these must be considered in respect to each child's interest and talent, as well as the parents' commitment to follow through.

Theater

Theater is naturally enriching, from the Greeks to Shakespeare to modern drama. Notwithstanding today's abuse of the medium, the theater remains a powerful means of creative expression.

Children often love live theater and light opera. So the main thing is to be selective and to take your children on occasion. Often small local plays offer the best in theme selection and audience involvement, and the price is right. A brief call to your local high schools, colleges, and drama troupes will provide too much to choose from. If the play has a serious theme, like *Peer Gynt,* read it first yourself. Then you can tell your children what to look for.

Don't rule out opera. Some operagoers consult the librettos (the opera text) before attending, but usually they read a short synopsis of the plot and music in a book like Milton Cross's *Complete Stories of the Great Operas*. This makes the opera so much more enjoyable if you're neophytes (as we are). We became hooked when a friend sang the lead in *La Sonnambula* at Chicago's Lyric Opera. Children *can* enjoy opera. We once had a ten-year-old neighbor who loved it!

Moving from the Lyric to the living room, we must not forget to mention family productions. Our experience has been more good laughs per minute than anything else!

Visual Arts

Painting and sculpture are often the first things that come to mind at the mention of art. Certainly the Lord has instilled these skills as a display of his creative image in humanity. Significantly, when we read God's directions for building both the tabernacle and the temple, we see that he commissioned *abstract art* (pure design), *representational art* (which represented something in nature or heaven), and *symbolic art* (the ark of the covenant being a prime example). And certain artists were specially gifted by the Spirit to carry out the commission.

The creative impulse, when skillfully executed, is humanly enriching. That is why a stroll down the halls of a great museum of art can be so elevating. Get to know your city's museum(s). Bring your children for visits of appropriate length and content so they will begin to be comfortable. Take them to sections and exhibitions that you know they will enjoy.

Hang your favorite prints on the walls of your home. Purchase books of the master artists, and leave them where your children can browse through them. Tack up unframed prints (framing is so expensive) in your children's bedrooms along with their posters. They will likely find themselves far more entranced by a Van Gogh or a Turner than by their sports heroes.

Also keep a supply of art and craft materials for your children's use. Post their creations, and be generous with your praise.

Movies

Whether we like it or not, movies have become the dominant art form of our time. Most movies are sub-Christian and bad art as well. But parents make a tactical mistake by limiting TV and cinema without providing attractive options. We recommend assembling a home video library. In the appendix on page 221 are some titles our family enjoyed, and we recommend them for older children and adults.

Because the arts have such power to enrich or debase, parents need to take charge. Guiding your children in respect to music, theater, painting and sculpture, and cinema requires time and hard work. But you can do it — and it's worth doing.

STORYTELLING

Historically, storytelling has been a primary source of family enrichment. Even where writing existed, oral tradition was often the main vehicle for passing along culture and family lore. Today, though storytelling has suffered from life's increased pace and the diminishing of conversation by the ever-present television, it can still be a major avenue of family enrichment. This happens in two ways: the relating of family history and wisdom, and the spinning of tales.

Mothers and fathers who labor to give their children a sense of their roots, an oral history of the personalities in the family, and a commentary on the lessons learned do their offspring a substantial favor. No doubt this most often happens on holidays or vacations when people are together and have time to listen. Sometimes storytelling can be stimulated by a family photo album or the "formal" use of a tape recorder for posterity. Wise parents will do well to orchestrate such times.

The spinning of yarns, whoppers that have only the slightest basis in reality, enriches relationships because they create a lore that is totally "family." When our children were small, we were watching a game show with Grandpa, and we had a great laugh at one of the contestant's names, Miss Bonita Hooker. As a family of fishermen, we recognized Bonita as the name of a Pacific game fish, and of course a hook is the hardware upon which fish are caught. So it was that Bonita Hooker became the protagonist for ridiculous family yarns most often spun as we traveled to Corona Del Mar for a day at the beach. The stories were funny to no one but us, but they served as humorous family glue.

When the time came to initiate our grandsons into the sublimities of bluegill fishing (and they are "hooked" devotees), we began to exchange fishing stories. Grandpa told a real story: "Boys, it was a cloudless day on the Coronada Islands . . ." Perhaps he used a little embroidery. And then the boys took turns telling their whoppers. Their eyes grew wide as they imagined — and what came out would tax the collective creativity of Jules Verne, Ernest Hemingway, and Isaac Asimov!

TRAVEL

Travel has been a long-standing mode of enrichment. In the past, it was naturally enriching because it was *slow*. Travelers moved at a snail's pace through countryside and cultures, talking to the people, examining their monuments, observing their lifestyles, and learning how they thought. Travel books were perennial best-sellers in the eighteenth and nineteenth centuries. A *Baedeker's Guide* (the popular guidebook series) was the symbol of travel and an enriched life.

But today travel is not automatically enriching. Often it means a ride to the airport, boarding and deplaning, and a quick taxi to a resort. Even in a car, we can speed through entire cultures, stopping only at gas stations and fast-food restaurants. This, of course, is perfectly fine if relaxation at a vacation spot is our only goal, and sometimes it ought to be.

Nevertheless, as children grow older, parents should give disciplined thought to planning *some* enriching vacations. Two simple guidelines can help make this happen. First, *choose enriching vacation spots* — national parks, historic locales, state and national capitals, and perhaps foreign countries. Second, parents must *plan the details* that will produce an enriching vacation. The cliché is ever true: "If you fail to plan, you plan to fail." Another good idea is to combine the two enrichments of travel and reading.

If you're planning a family tour of California, for example, you would do well to have someone read a brief history of California. Good supplements include one of the great California novels like Frank Norris's classic *The Octopus* (a terrific read!) or one of John Steinbeck's shorter novels like *The Red Pony* or *Of Mice and Men*. A visit to the Sierras, and Yosemite Valley especially, would be enriched by a reading of John Muir's *The Mountains of California*. In the Midwest, visiting the Laura Ingalls Wilder sites is a natural for families that have read the *Little House* series (a book entitled *Laura Ingalls Wilder Country* should be enough to whet anyone's anticipation for the venture). If you wonder where to find sites associated with favorite authors, or if you want to know which authors had connections in a region where you plan to travel, just use a search engine on the Internet.

We are not suggesting an uptight "Now, family, we must read Emily Dickinson before we get to Amherst" vacation. Obsessiveness will spoil the best of plans. Be flexible and relaxed. Our point is that *some* preparation as to history, geography, and literature can help make an enriching vacation. (The appendix on page 231 contains further information on vacation spots and their historical and literary connections.)

We realize that some traveling of this type, even though enriching, can be expensive. Some less costly travel ideas can work for your family's enrichment.

Travel to Your State Capital

State capitals are repositories of historical treasures and memorabilia and often outstanding architecture as well. They are always staffed with willing state employees whose job is to show you around. We live in the "Land of Lincoln"; Springfield is just 160 miles away, and it has public camping facilities. It takes several days to "do" Springfield. But it can be done without mortgaging the house.

Travel in Your City

Our home is only twenty-five miles west of Chicago; it is a thirty-five-minute drive. But we are repeatedly amazed by fellow suburbanites who tell us, "I never go into the city," as if it's a sign of their good sense. We think otherwise. Chicago has twenty-two art galleries, crowned by the renowned Art Institute of Chicago. It has around 150 museums, including the famed Field Museum of Natural History and the Museum of Science and Industry. The Chicago Historical Society has many of the treasures of the Midwest. There are sixty-plus theaters in the Windy City, including the highly regarded Goodman and Steppenwolf. The city has not only some of the tallest but the finest collection of large buildings in the world. There are five architectural tours available. Fine universities are on all sides, including the University of Chicago and its Oriental Institute.

In addition to this, there is the Lincoln Park Zoo, the Shedd Aquarium, the Garfield Park Conservatory, and Orchestra Hall with its national treasure, the Chicago Symphony Orchestra. All this, and a bevy of Frank Lloyd Wright homes in nearby Oak Park. Plus, there are some things few of us think of — the churches. We have made them our personal hobby!

Our point is this: You can have a huge travel experience and never leave the city that is nearest to you. Most people live close to a major city.

Travel in Your Home

Still too pricey? Here's a real deal: Travel to Austria, France, Kenya, Mexico, Guatemala, or Australia without ever leaving your home. Here's how: (1) choose your country, (2) prepare the country's cuisine, (3) play the country's music as background, (4) invite an acquaintance from that country to dine with you, and (5) show a travel video of the land.

Travel enriches. Parents need to choose wisely and plan well!

LANGUAGES

We have observed that learning a foreign language can be very enriching. Unfortunately, we did not cultivate a second language. If we had, Spanish would have been our choice because we were Californians with many Spanish-speaking friends and a love for Latin culture. Kent took four years of Spanish in high school and managed to get along in Southern Californian pidgin Spanish. Barbara studied Latin. And our children took other languages.

This was a missed opportunity for enrichment because a shared second language would have provided a common learning of customs, culture, and thought patterns. This would have enhanced our family exchange, vacations, and ministry.

But whether or not learning a language is something the whole family undertakes, you can start your children early on the mastery of a second language. They will thank you for it.

ENTERTAINING GUESTS

Among the most enriching things a family can do is to host travelers and visitors in the home. Over the years we have hosted famous writers, prominent theologians, a Russian ballerina, preachers and evangelists, and missionaries from around the world, as well as numerous international students. As a result, our children have sat in on hundreds of hours of stimulating conversation in which Dad and Mom were being stretched with new ideas and possibilities, while having their own vision for the world enlarged.

We cannot encourage strongly enough the ministry of hospitality to travelers. We know of some Christian families who, as a matter of biblical principle, wisely keep a "prophet's chamber" for guests — especially those who are traveling to proclaim the gospel (see 2 Kings 4:9-10). Don't wait until your home situation is perfect, for it never will be. Besides, if you do open your home to guests, you may find that you "have entertained angels unawares" (Heb. 13:2). Now *that* would be an enriching experience!

NATURE

Late in the afternoon, after a day of fishing off Cabo San Lucas, we dropped anchor in an emerald bay, donned snorkels, and slipped over the side into beauty unparalleled in our experience.

It was "useless," nonutilitarian beauty. In fact, until the invention of diving masks, no one had ever seen it clearly. Why had God made it? For our pleasure that day? Perhaps. But billions of other people will never see it. The reason that God made those shimmering forms, the yellows and aquamarines, the slowly waving grass, is because he is Creator and enjoys creating.

That night when we lifted our eyes from the phosphorous streaks of fish fleeing the boat's bow and gazed toward Polaris and the spring constellations, we saw only the faintest glimmers of their beauty. We could not see the planets ringed with color or the fires of Arcturus, but they were there. Again, why? Because the Creator was pleased to make them.

Annie Dillard muses, "You are God. You want to make a forest, something to hold the soil, lock up solar energy, and give off oxygen. Wouldn't it be simpler just to rough in a slab of chemicals, a green acre of goo?" Of course, but God chooses to do it with radiantly productive beauty. "A big elm in a single season might make us as many as *six million* leaves, wholly intricate, without budging an inch."[1]

God joyfully expresses himself in the natural creation. This grand truth is recorded from Genesis to Revelation and is substantiated a billionfold by the empirical evidence of the creation, which God first thought and then spoke into being. We can see God and his handiwork in creation. This is why the psalmist sings:

> *The heavens are telling the glory of God;*
> *and the firmament proclaims his handiwork.*
> *Day to day pours forth speech,*
> *and night to night declares knowledge . . .*
> *yet their voice goes out through all the earth,*
> *and their words to the end of the world.* — Ps. 19:1-2, 4, RSV

Because of this, common sense tells us that every believer ought to be awestruck by nature because it reflects something of God. Wonder is the condition of a healthy heart, and whatever we can do to enhance our children's wonder for God through creation will enrich their souls.

As a young mother, Barbara understood this implicitly and was disciplined about instilling it in our children. During the school year she consciously did it every morning when she drove through a desolate alley to drop the children off. The alley was in a declining neighborhood, and the residents used it as a dump. Barbara didn't want the rusting appliances and discarded furniture to be the children's last focus before school. So she would say, "I wonder what beautiful thing we will see today?" Without fail they would find something beautiful from God: a flower growing in an unlikely place or perhaps a fat robin with eggs. Once, to their joy, they discovered that a cat had used one of the cast-off sofas to give birth to kittens. So daily they would pause for maybe thirty seconds for a look. Our children saw, through their mother's persistence, the awesome fact that the Creator infuses his way into everything, even the ugly.

Learn to marvel with your children over a single flower's beauty and intricacy, and then the amazing varieties of flowers. Own a bird book for your area of the country. Learn some of their songs so you can give glory to God's extravagant creativity.

Be awestruck yourself by human life — the miracle of a baby. Wonder at the earth, wind, fire, and water of conception and the impending birth of a little brother or sister. Teach your children to sing about the miracle of new life. (The appendix on page 232 contains the text of Mary Rice Hopkins's "First Heartbeat.")

There are scores of things to do that will teach your children the awe and wonder of God. But as we have said, the key is for you to be awed yourself and then consciously convey it. Here are some good activities along these lines:

- An expedition to the natural history museum, or the zoo, or the aquarium, or the arboretum.
- Children love nature walks if you will do a little study and be the "expert."
- Invite a naturalist or geologist to accompany your family on an outing.
- Books on nature. There are hundreds!
- Nature videos.

PETS

We purposely allowed our children numerous pets, not because we were pet lovers, but because we believed that pets were enriching. There was a time when we simultaneously had an English bulldog, a large tomcat, a parrot, a parakeet, rabbits, hamsters, goldfish, desert tortoises, and a tarantula. Incidentally, all were inherited.

Pets are enriching because they teach responsibility. Animals must be fed and cleaned up after; some must be bathed, exercised, and groomed. Any child who is made to properly care for an animal will learn to be responsible.

Second, animals breed affection. Comedian Flip Wilson said he owned a bulldog to teach his children that "there could be a lot of good behind an ugly face." This was certainly true of our Precious. She was ugly — in an adorable kind of way. But she was lovingly devoted to the children, slapping them with a wet kiss from her long tongue whenever she got the chance. And the children loved her dearly, fighting to hold all sixty pounds of her like a baby or to cuddle with her.

Third, animals, especially baby animals, invite nurturing. We had our share of puppies, baby rats, and rabbits. So our boys and girls indulged in the natural tenderness and nursing that newborn creatures demand.

Fourth, pets invariably assist in teaching "the facts of life." When Holly, then five, bought herself a rat, she insisted that it was going to have babies. We sagely explained that this was impossible because it was necessary to have a "momma" and a "poppa." But she was unconvinced. Several days later Holly triumphantly announced that there were "babies." Indeed, there were — nine little pink critters, each about the size of an unusable piece of chalk. Now we had some explaining to do!

Animals also teach children the fact of death. All our longtime pets perished while our children were still at home, thereby demonstrating without a word the mortality of all living things. Thus they subtly learned something of their own mortality, a lesson that is a notable benefit in a death-denying culture. When we were forced to put our bulldog to sleep, Holly wrote, "I learned that love involved pain." An enriching piece of wisdom for a young teenager.

Pets are expensive even when they are free; they are inconvenient, messy, noisy, and demanding. But pets are enriching.

HOBBIES

Hobbies are thought by most to be synonymous with enrichment, though this view is subject to serious question. Hobbies, in fact, can be ruinous if they contradict the dictionary's trim definition: "an occupation of interest to which one gives his spare time." When the time hobbies occupy is no longer *spare*, the hobby becomes harmful. Hobbies also may be a problem if they become too costly, bring bad company, or become obsessive or overly competitive. To be enriching, a hobby should be enjoyable, relaxing, enlarging, and reserved for one's spare time.

Fishing has been that for Kent, who came to fishing through his mother. Grandfather Bray, a sportsman, disappeared in 1927, leaving a wife and two little girls — and a collection of fishing rods and guns. Kent's mother — one of those two little girls — later taught him and his brother what she knew of Grandpa's skills with rainbow trout on the Eel River, using salmon eggs and worms as bait. When Kent was a boy, there was hardly a day that he did not imagine a trout stream.

As Kent grew older, his tastes grew up. He came to understand that fishing was, in Geoffrey Norman's words, a matter of "slipping unobtrusively into the great chain of life and predation and living briefly by those ancient terms."[2] As a man, Kent came to further understand that the ultimate is doing it with an artificial fly! So now he dreams of an Orvis five-weight Far and Fine and Quill Gordons.

But fishing is always slipping unobtrusively into the great chain of life, whether with a worm or a Light Cahill. Our sons, one of our daughters, and our grandsons all share the thrill of "living briefly by those ancient terms." With our grandsons, it is a matter of a coffee can full of freshly dug worms, a Kmart spinning outfit, a bobber, and charging bluegill. Kent's hobby not only relaxes him but has given him a bond with some of his nearest and dearest.

The list of hobbies covers an endless range: stamp collecting, gardening, woodworking, sewing, photography, pottery, model building, painting. Each hobby has its own lore, its own mystery, and its own singular pleasures that are impossible to communicate to the uninitiated (who may, however, choose to be initiated if they wish).

Hobbies are enlarging and enriching. They keep us interested, and they make us more interesting. Be tolerant of your children's side interests, even their eccentricities. They may become great family treasures.

SKILLS

We know that women can learn to do what has traditionally been called men's work (fix a tire) and that men can learn to do so-called women's work (sew on a button). But today we have men and women who know how to do neither!

Some of the problem arises from the unfortunate division of high school students into two groups: those who are going to college and those who are not. The college-bound hit the books, and the vocation-bound hit the manual arts: machine shop, sewing, auto mechanics, cooking, and woodworking, to name a few. Our system has produced educated people who can't fix a light switch or paint a wall. This is an impoverished state.

Schooling aside, the answer is that these things ought to be learned in the home. The best way is to involve your teenage children in doing them. Are you painting and wallpapering a room? Include your children in the process. If they balk, *demand* this involvement, explaining that it is "for their own good" (a rationale they will not buy but that is nevertheless true). Don't make the mistake, however, of *overinvolving* them, demanding that they help with every decorating or fix-it project or expecting their enthusiasm to parallel yours. Follow the same procedure in other projects: minor plumbing repairs, fixing a toilet, unplugging the garbage disposal, re-siding the garage, bricking the porch, sewing on buttons, repairing rips in clothes, preparing meals, maintaining the car, changing the oil, changing a tire. Involve *both* your sons and daughters.

COOKING

Another skill that we believe is crucial is handiness in the kitchen. When our son Kent was in the fourth grade, he daily came home frustrated and angry from the pressures of school. Eager to find something he could enjoy without adding yet more stress to his life, Barbara found the solution in the kitchen. She allowed young Kent to take over her kitchen when he came home from school and bake cookies all by himself. She helped him only if he asked about a measurement or where to find an ingredient; otherwise, she stayed out of the way. She did not complain about spilled milk or flour dusting on every possible surface. Here was something Kent could do without criticism, receiving only praise for the yummy finished product.

And bake he did! By the time we moved to Illinois, Kent had become so proficient at baking cookies that he became the family cookie baker. He baked so many cookies over the years that when he left for college, Barbara said she had lost not only her baker but also her touch.

The kitchen has much to contribute to a family's well-being and heritage. Savory aromas from treasured recipes handed down from previous generations or given by former neighbors conjure pleasurable memories.

Everyone in our family knows that we use dill pickles rather than sweet pickles in our potato salad, and we put cinnamon but *never* nutmeg in our apple pie. Why? Because that's how Grandma did it. It doesn't taste right any other way!

We have observed that though our kitchen is the smallest room in the house, everyone congregates there at the end of the day. There is something about the preparation of a meal that draws us together. Hunger is certainly the key motivation! But there is more — being together, hovering over the boiling pot, inhaling the aroma of sautéing onions, the warmth, the expectation. It's good. It's right.

Our son Carey told us that he became aware of what a privilege it is to have grown up in a home where meals are special when he brought his college roommate home for Christmas. After the rest of us were in bed, Tim and Carey stayed up late talking in the kitchen. Periodically they would open the refrigerator door, take out some leftovers, and nibble on them. Late that night Tim opened the refrigerator once again and stood staring at its contents. "You don't know how lucky you are," he said to Carey. Since that Christmas, whenever our son returns home, opens the refrigerator, and looks at its *home-cooked* contents, he is thankful.

All of our children are comfortable in the kitchen. Our daughters are at ease, of course, because they are married, and cooking daily has increased their skill. But our children all gained the confidence to cook from observing how to chop an onion, prepare salad greens, and frost a cake. They have inherited their love for a good meal from the pleasant memories associated with the kitchens of their parents and grandparents, and they want to pass on the pleasure.

In this fast-food world, your children will not learn to appreciate the kitchen unless you do. Becoming a good cook is enriching. In fact, over the years your children will bless you for it. And so will their spouses! (The appendix on page 233 lists a few of our family's favorite recipes.)

ATHLETICS

Athletics are intrinsically enriching and important to a child's development — and at the same time highly overrated.

Athletic involvement is naturally enriching because it teaches discipline, teamwork, toughness, concentration, and competition. It also builds bodily strength, beauty, grace, and confidence. And it provides leisure, camaraderie, and entertainment. For these reasons we encouraged our children's participation in sports and were involved in coaching.

Ideally, it is best for a child to learn a *team* sport and an *individual* sport. Involvement in team sports tends to diminish after one's education, while individual sports become increasingly important. Witness the enduring popularity of golf, tennis, skiing, sailing, and fishing.

Athletic involvement can be wonderfully enriching if it is not an extension of the parents' "wanna-be" egos. While coaching, we have had to tell parents to be quiet or leave because they rode their kids mercilessly during a game. Our sense was that they had never made it themselves, and by gum their children *would* make it, no matter what.

Athletic involvement is also good if it follows a child's natural talent and interests. We recall a little guy who, during a soccer game, was paying no attention to the ball. As his teammates charged by, he obliviously skipped along counting the bees in the clover! Maybe his interest would develop someday, but this was not the time to force him to play soccer. Athletic activities are likewise good if they are a *part* of life, but not its sum total. Unfortunately, some coaches believe that every team member must be convinced that his or her sport involvement is the most important thing in life. Moreover, it is possible for either a team sport or an individual sport to occupy more time than the rest of schooling. This is educational and spiritual insanity — even if the child is the one in ten thousand who has a chance of making a living in athletics.

Parents, athletics can be profoundly enriching. But so much of it depends on your values and attitude.

ENRICHING LIFE

We have given a daunting list of ways to enrich your children's lives: *reading, arts, storytelling, travel, languages, guests, nature, pets, hobbies, skills, cooking,* and *athletics*. In providing this extensive list, we have created a danger — the idea that you must now implement everything under each heading if your children are to have an enriched life. Nothing could be further from the truth or our intentions.

We are writing from a decades-long perspective of our parenting career. Much of what we have listed took place at different times over the years. And you must also understand that we did not do everything mentioned in the categories. Some of the ideas come from other families or are the practical extension of the principle we were teaching. Regard it as an expanded list of ideas and resources from which to choose as you work at enriching your children's lives.

Don't attempt to do too much. Don't overprogram your life. Relax and enjoy your family. You'll always be an imperfect parent — so be a fun one. Enjoy life's arias. You'll be hearing the angels soon enough!

FOOD FOR THOUGHT

Why is it important to teach our children to be readers of wholesome materials? What competition do we face here, and how can we overcome it?

Why do we need to inculcate in our children a love for and interest in the arts? Music, theater, visual arts, movies—which are most appreciated in your home?

What are the values of storytelling? How can we regain or maintain this in our homes?

What can God for your family through nature? How can you help your children learn to marvel over the beauties of God's creation?

How can you help your children identify and develop the particular skills God has given them? How can we avoid their thinking that certain skills are for women or for women? How can we help them see that using their skills can be wonderful ministry for God and others?

AFTERWORD

Our childrearing years are over; our immediate family album is complete. It will not be long until the photographs become artifacts, curiosities from the distant past. We hope the potential written on each face will have been realized.

Of course, as we write, the voyage has not ended for us or our children. There are miles to go and uncharted seas to cross. But our children's sails are set. Every sailor knows that you can't sail without wind. Tacking into the wind is what helps you sail well. Our children will not sail with culture, but they can thrive with the tension of a healthy tack. We are aware that this represents the grace of God.

Our children are beginning their own family albums, and what bright faces they display! They are all in for a daunting journey because the culture of a soul is, as we have said, a wild ride.

No part of their voyage will be without difficulties because they, like their parents and their parents before them, are sinners and live in a fallen and sometimes tragic world. Nevertheless, if they live under Christ and the authority of his Word, cultivating the disciplines of heritage, attitudes, affection, traditions, spirituality, prayer, ministry, self-regard, discipline, manners, and enrichments, they will sail well.

Disciplines of a Godly Family has been a celebration of God's grace in the Christian family. It is our prayer that it will help prepare you for a graced voyage.

Appendix

AIDS TO CHRISTIAN EDUCATION
FOR USE IN THE FAMILY

Background books: Every Christian family would profit from a library with some basic recommended books such as: ed. J. D. Douglas, *The New Bible Dictionary*; ed. J. D. Douglas, *The New International Dictionary of the Christian Church*; J. Strong, *Strong's Exhaustive Concordance to the Bible*; Orville J. Nave, *Nave's Topical Bible* and *The Treasury of Scripture Knowledge*; Wayne Grudem, *Systematic Theology*. Along with these basic research tools, families should invest in a multi-volumed Bible commentary such as *The Expositor's Bible Commentary, The Tyndale Commentary,* or *The New International Commentary.*

Other printed aids: *The Westminster Shorter Catechism*; David Helm, *The Big Picture Book of the Bible.*

Internet sites such as Matthias Media (www.matthiasmedia.com.au), CBMW (Council on Biblical Manhood and Womanhood) (www.cbmw.com), Desiring God Ministries (John Piper) (www.desiring-god.org), Focus on the Family (www.family.org), and FamilyLife (www.familylife.com).

Flash cards of biblical vocabulary: We suggest you make your own cards of biblical terms that may be new to you or your children, such as: atonement, sacrifice, propitiation, mercy, tabernacle, redemption, sanctification, etc.

Bible memory programs.
Bible software programs.

ADVENT TREE
INSTRUCTIONS

For to us a child is born, to us a son is given, and the government
shall be upon his shoulder, and his name shall be called
Wonderful Counselor, Mighty God, Everlasting Father,
Prince of Peace.
ISAIAH 9:6

The story of Christmas actually began before God created the world. It was already in God's mind that he would send his only Son to earth to be born in Bethlehem and then later to die to save us from our sins. So God was working all through history to prepare for that first Christmas. The Bible tells the wonderful story of how God prepared the way for the coming of the Christ-child. These Advent family devotionals follow the whole Christmas story, from the very beginning when God created the world, right up to the birth of Jesus in a cattle shed. You may wish to use them in your family to remind you of God's wise and loving plan and to cause you to marvel even more at the blessing of salvation.

As a visual aid to these daily devotionals, we suggest making a Jesse Tree and hanging appropriate symbols from its branches. Simply go into the garden or your yard and clip a bare branch from a tree or shrub. Secure it upright in a clay pot. Then each day have your children create (color, paint, sew, etc.) the suggested symbol as ornaments to hang on the tree, making them as simple or elaborate as your family chooses. We used only construction paper and glue; others have cut out three- or four-inch circles of paper or cardboard and let the children draw the symbols on them. If you want to get fancy, you can also use sequins, glitter, gold braid, and the like, but such additions are certainly not necessary. Use your imagination![1]

DAY 1:
THE LIGHT OF CREATION

Scriptures

Genesis 1:1; John 1:1-5.

Special Verse

"In the beginning, God created the heavens and the earth." *Genesis 1:1*

Questions

- What did God create? (Name some things God created.)
- Who was with God in the beginning?
- Who is the light of men and our light? (Talk about traditions and decorations that symbolize God's creations and Jesus, our light.)

Prayer

Heavenly Father, you are so great and good. You made the world and everything around us. Thank you for showing your love to us in creation and in Jesus, our perfect light! As we see Christmas lights this season, may we be reminded of the true and perfect light that lit up the world that first Christmas. Amen.

Symbol for Jesse Tree Ornament

Rising sun on horizon with rays of light.

DAY 2:
THE FIRST SIN

Scriptures

Genesis 3:1-10, 23; Isaiah 53:6; Romans 5:8.

Special Verse

"All we like sheep have gone astray, we have turned every one to his own way." *Isaiah 53:6*

Questions

- Did Adam and Eve obey God? Why not?
- What is sin?
- Are you sinful? How do you know?
- How did God show his love in spite of our sin?

Prayer

Holy God, we sin against you every day. Please forgive us through your Son, Jesus, who came to earth to die for us. Help us to obey and follow you. Help us to forgive others as you forgive us. Thank you for forgiving us and washing us clean. Amen.

Symbol for Jesse Tree Ornament

Apple and snake.

DAY 3:
INSIDE THE ARK

Scriptures

Genesis 6:5-8; 7:17-23; Romans 6:23.

Special Verse

"For the wages of sin is death, but the free gift of God is eternal life in Christ Jesus our Lord." *Romans 6:23*

Questions

- Why did God send the Flood?
- Was anyone saved besides those on the ark?
- What does everyone deserve?
- What is God's gift?

Prayer

Lord, you are faithful to your promises. You love us so much that you offer eternal life to us as a free gift through the greatest gift, Christ Jesus, our Lord. Help us to remember your precious gift during this Christmas season. Amen.

Symbol for Jesse Tree Ornament

Noah's ark, or a rainbow.

DAY 4:
THE CALL TO ABRAM

Scriptures

Genesis 12:1-7.

Special Verse

"In you all the families of the earth shall be blessed." *Genesis 12:3*

Questions

- Why did Abram leave his home?
- What were God's promises to Abram?
- How did Abram respond to God's commands and promises?

Prayer

Dear Lord, give us faith like Abram had. Help us to obey your commands, whether they seem hard or easy. Let us follow your Son, Jesus, who was completely obedient to you. Thank you for already giving us the perfect blessing in the long-promised Jesus. Show us ways to bless others. Amen.

Symbol for Jesse Tree Ornament

A tent.

DAY 5:
ISAAC AND THE LAMB

Scriptures

Genesis 22:1-13; John 1:29.

Special Verse

"Behold, the Lamb of God, who takes away the sin of the world!" *John 1:29*

Questions

- What very hard thing did God tell Abraham to do?
- What does it mean to make a sacrifice?
- Tell one hard thing God has asked you to do.
- Did Abraham obey?
- Who is the sacrifice for your sins?

Prayer

Dear Jesus, thank you for dying on the cross for my sins. Thank you for obeying your Father and doing this very hard thing for me. Thank you, God, for giving your only Son. Please help me to obey you when you ask me to do a hard thing. We love you, Lamb of God, who takes away our sins. Amen.

Symbol for Jesse Tree Ornament

A lamb.

DAY 6:
JACOB'S LADDER

Scriptures

Genesis 28:10-17.

Special Verse

"I am with you and will keep you wherever you go." *Genesis 28:15*

Questions

- What was Jacob's pillow for the night?
- What did Jacob see in his dream?
- What did God promise Jacob?
- Why did Jacob call the place of his dream an "awesome" place?

Prayer

Dear Lord, thank you that you never sleep but always stay awake watching us and protecting us. Help us to remember that you can see us *anywhere* we go. You watched over Jacob sleeping on his stone and the baby Jesus sleeping in Bethlehem, and you watch over us whether we're asleep or awake. Thank you, God, for being our faithful friend. Amen.

Symbol for Jesse Tree Ornament

A ladder.

DAY 7:
JOSEPH'S COAT OF MANY COLORS

Scriptures

Genesis 37:3-36; 50:18-21; Romans 8:28.

Special Verse

"And we know that for those who love God all things work together for good." *Romans 8:28*

Questions

• What happened to Jacob's family when he loved one son more than the others?

• How did Joseph's brothers feel about him? Why? What did they do?

• What did Joseph know about God and his plan that helped him to forgive his brothers?

• Have you forgiven someone who hurt you?

• Sing together "He's Got the Whole World in His Hands."

Prayer

Dear heavenly Father, thank you that you have the whole world and every person in your hands. You planned the coming of your Son to save us, and you are watching over us as we live each day. Please help us to trust you when things don't work out the way we want them to. Take away any worry or jealousy or hate we have in our hearts today. Thank you for forgiving us over and over again. Amen.

Symbol for Jesse Tree Ornament

A many-colored coat.

DAY 8:
MOSES AND THE TEN COMMANDMENTS

Scriptures

Exodus 20:1-20; 32:15-16; Psalm 119:11.

Special Verse

"I have stored up your word in my heart, that I might not sin against you." *Psalm 119:11*

Questions

- What was written on the stone tablets?
- Who gave these laws to Moses?
- How many of the Ten Commandments can you remember?
- Why do God and our parents give us rules?
- What can we do with God's Word that will help keep us from sinning?
- Memorize Psalm 119:11.

Prayer

Dear God, thank you for writing us a very special letter. The Bible is very important to us because it is from you. Please help us to read it and memorize it; but most of all, help us to *obey* it. We know that you have given us rules for our own good because you know what's best for us. Thank you that in the Bible we can read all about how you sent your Son, Jesus, to us. We will hide your Word in our hearts. Amen.

Symbol for Jesse Tree Ornament

Tablets with Hebrew letters — the Ten Commandments.

Day 9:
Canaan, the Promised Land of Blessings

Scriptures

Numbers 13:1-2, 17-23, 27; Psalm 103:2.

Special Verse

"Bless the LORD, O my soul, and forget not all his benefits." *Psalm 103:2*

Questions

- Would Canaan be a good land to live in? Why or why not?
- Did God want to bless the people by giving them this land?
- Does God want to bless you?
- What are some of his blessings to you?

Prayer

Dear Lord, thank you so much for the many ways you bless us. (Have individual family members thank God for particular blessings to them.) Help us never to forget your goodness. Thank you most of all for our greatest blessing, your Son, Jesus, who came to earth on that first Christmas. Amen.

Symbol for Jesse Tree Ornament

A cluster of grapes.

DAY 10:
RUTH AND BOAZ

Scriptures

Ruth 1:14-18; 2:4-18; 4:13-16.

Special Verse

"Your people shall be my people, and your God my God." *Ruth 1:16*

Questions

• Why do you think Ruth wanted to leave her homeland and family?

• What things had Boaz heard about Ruth?

• How did God reward Ruth?

Prayer

Lord, help us to love and desire you the way Ruth did. Help us not only to think of ourselves, but even more, to follow Ruth's example in serving others. Thank you that your Son, Jesus, was willing to leave heaven and come to earth for us. Help us most of all to be like him. Amen.

Symbol for Jesse Tree Ornament

Wheat.

DAY 11:
KING DAVID

Scriptures

1 Samuel 17:1-9, 32-50; Psalm 23:1.

Special Verse

"The LORD is my shepherd; I shall not want." *Psalm 23:1*

Questions

- Describe what Goliath looked like and how he acted.
- Why did David fight Goliath?
- Do you think David felt afraid? Why or why not?
- Why did David win?

Prayer

Lord, we praise you for your might and power. Help us to remember how strong you are when we feel afraid of other people. Help us to be bold in telling others how you sent your Son to die for us. Thank you that you will always protect us like a shepherd protects his sheep. Amen.

Symbol for Jesse Tree Ornament

A slingshot.

DAY 12:
JOSIAH FINDS THE LAW

Scriptures

2 Kings 22:11-13; 23:1-3; Psalm 119:105.

Special Verse

"Your word is a lamp to my feet and a light to my path." *Psalm 119:105*

Questions

- What had happened to God's Word before Josiah's time?
- What did King Josiah do when he found the book?
- Why should we read the Bible?

Prayer

Dear Father, thank you for your guidebook, the Bible. Thank you for the way it tells us about yourself, us, and our world — and especially about Jesus. Help us to follow your words in all we do and say this Christmas season. Amen.

Symbol for Jesse Tree Ornament

A parchment.

DAY 13:
PROPHECY OF THE SHOOT FROM THE
STUMP OF JESSE

Scriptures

Isaiah 11:1-5; John 1:14.

Special Verse

"The Word became flesh and dwelt among us, and we have seen his glory." *John 1:14*

Questions

• Jesse was the father of David, from whose descendants came Jesus Christ. How is Jesse like a stump, and who is the new branch growing out of him?

• Who is full of grace, truth, wisdom, understanding, power, righteousness, and faithfulness?

• How did Isaiah know about Jesus hundreds of years before he was born?

• How is Jesus God's living Word?

Prayer

Thank you, God, for promising your Son long ago. Thank you that he came and showed us what you are like. Please help us to be more like Jesus every day. Amen.

Symbol for Jesse Tree Ornament

A tree stump with a green leaf growing out of the top.

DAY 14:
PROPHECY OF THE LION AND LAMB
RESTING TOGETHER

Scriptures

Isaiah 11:6-10.

Special Verse

"The wolf shall dwell with the lamb, and the leopard shall lie down with the young goat, the calf and the lion and the fattened calf together; and a little child shall lead them." *Isaiah 11:6*

Questions

- Will all the animals on earth be tame enough to pet someday?
- Why will this happen?
- When will this happen?

Prayer

Thank you, Jesus, that you came the first time, on Christmas. Thank you that you will come again and make our world safe from evil and harm. We praise you for this promise of a new world. Help us obey you, learn your ways, and trust that we will be part of the new world, through Jesus our Savior. Amen.

Symbol for Jesse Tree Ornament

Lion and lamb together.

DAY 15:
PROPHECY OF THE PRINCE OF PEACE

Scriptures

Isaiah 9:6-7; John 14:27.

Special Verse

"Peace I leave with you; my peace I give to you. Not as the world gives do I give to you. Let not your hearts be troubled, neither let them be afraid." *John 14:27*

Questions

- What different names is Jesus called in these verses?
- In what ways does this world need a Prince of Peace?
- What things trouble you? Can Jesus bring peace to *you*?

Prayer

Thank you, Jesus, for being our Prince of Peace. Help us not to be troubled or afraid, but to be filled with your peace. Help us to bring your peace to our troubled world. Amen.

Symbol for Jesse Tree Ornament

A dove and a crown.

DAY 16:
PROPHECY OF A GENTLE SHEPHERD

Scriptures

Isaiah 40:11; Psalm 23:1-2; John 10:27.

Special Verse

"My sheep hear my voice, and I know them, and they follow me."
John 10:27

Questions

• What are several different ways in which shepherds care for their sheep?

• How are we like sheep?

• What must Jesus be like if he is our shepherd?

Prayer

Gentle Shepherd, thank you for always taking care of us and guiding us back into your loving arms. Thank you for healing our hurts and protecting us from our enemies. Help us listen to your voice and follow your call. Amen.

Symbol for Jesse Tree Ornament

A shepherd's crook and a lamb.

DAY 17:
PROPHECY OF THE SUFFERING SERVANT

Scriptures

Isaiah 53; John 10:14-15.

Special Verse

"And I lay down my life for the sheep." *John 10:15*

Questions

- What was God's plan for Jesus? Why is it important that Jesus died?
- Why was Jesus willing to die? Have you given your life to Jesus?

Prayer

Heavenly Father, thank you for sending your Son, Jesus, to die in our place as payment for our sins. What a perfect "Christmas gift" — your Son and eternal life with you forever. Help us to accept this gift and to give our life to you. Help us also to share this gift with others through our actions and our words. Amen.

Words to Ponder

> *Children, can you tell me why*
> *Jesus came to bleed and die?*
> *He was happy high above,*
> *Dwelling in His Father's love,*
> *Yet He left His joy and bliss,*
> *For a wicked world like this.*
> *We were all by sin undone,*
> *Yet He loved us ev'ry one;*
> *So to earth He kindly came,*
> *On the cross to bear our shame,*
> *And to wash away our guilt*
> *In the precious blood He spilt.* — *Author Unknown*

Symbol for Jesse Tree Ornament

A cross.

DAY 18:
PROPHECY OF THE NEW COVENANT

Scriptures

Jeremiah 31:31-34; Hebrews 9:13-15; Acts 16:31.

Special Verse

"I will put my law within them, and I will write it on their hearts. And I will be their God, and they will be my people." *Jeremiah 31:33*

Questions

- A covenant is a _____.
  a. law
  b. promise
  c. teaching
- Do people always keep their promises? Has anyone ever broken a promise to you?
  - Does God always keep his promises?
  - What does God promise in these verses?
  - How should we respond to these promises?

Prayer

Dear Father, thank you that your Son forgives us and lives in us when we believe in him. May Jesus in us write your law on our minds and hearts. Thank you that if Christ is in our hearts, you remember our sins no more. We trust your promises, O God. Amen.

Symbol for Jesse Tree Ornament

A heart.

DAY 19:
THE EXILE

Scriptures

Daniel 3:19-29; Jeremiah 1:8.

Special Verse

"Do not be afraid of them, for I am with you to deliver you." *Jeremiah 1:8*

Questions

• What did Shadrach, Meshach, and Abednego refuse to do?

• What punishment did Nebuchadnezzar order because of their refusal?

• How many men did the king see walking in the fire?

• How did God provide for Shadrach, Meshach, and Abednego?

Prayer

Dear Lord, give us strength to say no when we are tempted to do things against you, especially when we are surrounded by those who do not believe in you. Help us not to be afraid, for you are with us and will rescue us. This Christmas season, help us to be bold to stand up for you in all we say and do. Amen.

Symbol for Jesse Tree Ornament

A fiery furnace.

DAY 20:
THE RETURN TO THE LAND

Scriptures

Nehemiah 1:3; 2:17-18; 6:15-16; 8:10.

Special Verse

"The joy of the LORD is your strength." *Nehemiah 8:10*

Questions

 • What happened to the wall around Jerusalem after the Jews were captured and exiled in Babylon?
 • Who enabled Nehemiah and the people to rebuild the wall?
 • How did the surrounding people feel?

Prayer

Thank you, God, for bringing Nehemiah and his people back to the Promised Land, where the Messiah would be born. We praise you for your mighty power in accomplishing your purposes so that your enemies tremble. Show your power in our lives this Christmas. Amen.

Words to Ponder

> *What can I give Him,*
> *Poor as I am?*
> *If I were a shepherd,*
> *I would bring a lamb.*
> *If I were a wise man,*
> *I would do my part.*
> *Yet what I can I give Him:*
> *Give my heart.* — *Christina Rossetti*

Symbol for Jesse Tree Ornament

A wall of bricks.

DAY 21:
PROPHECY OF BETHLEHEM

Scriptures

Isaiah 7:14; Micah 5:2; Luke 2:1-7.

Special Verse

"But you, O Bethlehem Ephrathah, who are too little to be among the clans of Judah, from you shall come forth for me one who is to be ruler in Israel." *Micah 5:2*

Questions

   • What did the Old Testament prophets know ahead of time about Jesus' birth?
      • How did they know?
      • How long ahead of time did God know about Jesus' birth?

Prayer

Dear God, thank you for planning long, long ago to send your Son to save us. You even planned what little town he would be born in. Thank you that you have good plans for each of your children. We trust your loving plans for us. Amen.

Symbol for Jesse Tree Ornament

A picture of the village of Bethlehem.

DAY 22:
THE LIGHT OF THE WORLD

Scriptures

Luke 1:26-38; 2:25-32; John 8:12.

Special Verse

"I am the light of the world. Whoever follows me will not walk in darkness." *John 8:12*

Questions

- What good news did the angel Gabriel deliver to Mary?
- How did Mary react to this news?
- How did Gabriel describe Jesus?
- How did Simeon describe Jesus?
- How can you be a light for Jesus in the world?

Prayer

Thank you, God, for Mary's willingness to be the mother of Jesus and to let his light shine through her. We praise you as the Light of the World and the light of our life. May your light shine through us to help light the way for many others. Amen.

Symbol for Jesse Tree Ornament

A candle with flame.

DAY 23:
THE BIRTH OF JESUS

Scriptures

Luke 2:1-7; John 3:16-17.

Special Verse

"For God so loved the world, that he gave his only Son, that whoever believes in him should not perish but have eternal life." *John 3:16*

Questions

- Who sent Jesus into the world?
- Where did Jesus live before he came to earth?
- Why did Jesus come to earth?
- Do you believe in him?

Prayer

Dear Father God, thank you for sending your Son to our world to save us. You planned it long ago, you made it happen just at the right time, and now we look back with wonder at that first Christmas. Come into our heart *this* Christmas, dear Savior. Amen.

Words to Ponder

> *Little baby in a manger,*
> *You came to earth a tiny stranger,*
> *But soon the world would know*
> *You'd give the greatest gift of love.*
> *You came to earth to die on Calvary*
> *Bear the pain and shame to die for me.*
> *I can't believe it — but it's so.*
>
> *For you gave up your throne in glory.*
> *All the pow'r of the world was in your hands.*
> *You gave up your right to be ruler,*
> *You gave it up — just to be a man.*
>
> *Your kingdom was not to be worldly,*
> *Even tho' you could reign throughout the land.*
> *Your glory grew dim as a baby,*
> *And it was all a part of God's plan.*
>
> *Little baby in a manger,*
> *You came to earth a tiny stranger.*
> *I found a home for you today;*
> *Come in my heart and always stay.* — *Dean Lambert*

Symbol for Jesse Tree Ornament

A manger scene.

DAY 24:
ANGELS PROCLAIM THE COMING OF CHRIST

Scriptures

Hebrews 1:14; Luke 2:8-20; Psalm 91:9-12.

Special Verse

"Glory to God in the highest, and on earth peace among those with whom he is pleased." *Luke 2:14*

Questions

- What was the angels' message to the shepherds?
- What different reactions did the shepherds have to the angels?
- For whose sake are angels sent?
- Do you think angels help protect you?

Prayer

Thank you, God, for your ministering servants, the angels. Thank you for their joyful message that first Christmas. And thank you that in so many different ways you guard us, protect us, and proclaim to us your joy. Amen.

Symbol for Jesse Tree Ornament

An angel.

DAY 25:
THE STAR

Scriptures

Matthew 2:1-12; Revelation 22:16.

Special Verse

"When they saw the star, they rejoiced exceedingly with great joy."
Matthew 2:10

Questions

- Who saw Jesus' star in the east, and what did they want?
- Did King Herod want to worship Jesus?
- Where did the star come to rest?
- How is Jesus described in Revelation 22:16?
- How is Jesus like a star?

Prayer

Father, thank you for showing your love for the whole world when you sent your bright Morning Star to shine on us. Just as the wise men were overjoyed, let us be filled with joy by your presence with us. Light the path ahead of us, we pray, all the way to heaven. Amen.

Words to Ponder

> *The wise may bring their learning,*
> *The rich may bring their wealth,*
> *And some may bring their greatness,*
> *And some their strength and health;*
> *We too would bring our treasures*
> *To offer to the king;*
> *We have no wealth or learning:*
> *What shall we children bring?*
> *We'll bring Him hearts that love Him;*
> *We'll bring Him thankful praise,*
> *And young souls meekly striving*
> *To walk in holy ways:*
> *And these shall be the treasures*
> *We offer to the King,*
> *And these are gifts that even*
> *The poorest child may bring.* — *Author Unknown*

Symbol for Jesse Tree Ornament

A star.

Good Christian Men, Rejoice

Good Christian men, rejoice with heart and soul and voice;

Give ye heed to what we say: News! news! Jesus Christ is born today!

Ox and ass before Him bow, and He is in the manger now.

Christ is born today! Christ is born today!

Good Christian men, rejoice with heart and soul and voice;

Now ye hear of endless bliss: Joy! joy!

Jesus Christ was born for this!

He has opened heaven's door, and man is blessed evermore.

Christ was born for this! Christ was born for this!

Good Christian men, rejoice with heart and soul and voice;

Now ye need not fear the grave: Peace! peace!

Jesus Christ was born to save!

Calls you one and calls you all to gain His everlasting hall.

Christ was born to save! Christ was born to save!

LATIN CAROL — TRANSLATED BY JOHN M. NEALE

RESOURCES FOR CELEBRATING A CHRISTIAN PASSOVER

Several books have been written about the significance of Passover for Christians. Here are three that should be available through your local Christian bookstore (or you can order them from Jews for Jesus).

Christ in the Passover, by Moishe and Ceil Rosen (Moody Press, 1978), tells how the seder was celebrated by the Jews in Jesus' time and shows how Christ's atoning work relates to the Passover.

Celebrate Passover Haggadah: A Christian Celebration of the Traditional Jewish Festival, by Joan R. Lipis (Purple Pomegranate Productions, 1993), lays out the seder celebration clearly and completely, especially for Christians. The actual order of service, the preparations, the responsive readings, and Passover music are included.

Passover Haggadah: A Messianic Celebration, by Eric-Peter Lipson (Purple Pomegranate, 1986), provides the traditional Passover blessings, in both Hebrew and English, as well as the music for Passover songs.

You may also want to talk to your pastor about having your church host a *Christ in the Passover* presentation by a Jews for Jesus missionary. You can obtain more information about this program by contacting Jews for Jesus, Dept. of Mobile Evangelism, 60 Haight Street, San Francisco, CA 94102, phone: (415) 864-2600.

GOVERNOR WILLIAM BRADFORD'S
Thanksgiving Proclamation, 1623

To all ye Pilgrims

INASMUCH as the great Father has given us this year an abundant harvest of Indian corn, wheat, beans, squashes, and garden vegetables, and has made the forests to abound with game and the sea with fish and clams, and inasmuch as He has protected us from the ravages of the savages, has spared us from pestilence and disease, has granted us freedom to worship God according to the dictates of our conscience; now, I, your magistrate, do proclaim that all ye Pilgrims, with your wives and little ones, do gather at ye meeting house, on ye hill, between the hours of 9 and 12 in the day time, on Thursday, November ye 29th of the year of our Lord one thousand six hundred and twenty-three, and the third year since ye Pilgrims landed on ye Pilgrim Rock, there to listen to ye pastor, and render thanksgiving to ye Almighty God for all His blessings.

A Puritan Prayer for Thanksgiving

O MY GOD,
Thou fairest, greatest, first of all objects,
our hearts admire, adore, love thee,
for our little vessels are as full as they can be,
and we would pour out all that fulness before thee in ceaseless flow.

When we think upon and converse with thee
ten thousand delightful thoughts spring up,
ten thousand sources of pleasure are unsealed,
ten thousand refreshing joys spread over our hearts,
crowding into every moment of happiness.

We bless thee for the soul thou hast created,
for adorning it, sanctifying it, though it is fixed in barren soil;
for the body thou hast given us,
for preserving its strength and vigour;
for the ease and freedom of our limbs,
for hands, eyes, ears that do thy bidding;
for thy royal bounty providing our daily support,
for a full table and overflowing cup,
for appetite, taste, sweetness,
for social joys of relatives and friends,
for ability to serve others,
for hearts that feel sorrows and necessities,
for minds to care for our fellow men,
for opportunities of spreading happiness around,
for loved ones in the joys of heaven,
for our own expectations of seeing thee clearly.

We love thee above the powers of language to express,
for what thou art to thy creatures.
Increase our love, O our God, through time and eternity.

Two Ways to Live

This appendix is a condensed version of a Matthias Media publication called *Two Ways to Live* and is used with permission (http://www.matthiasmedia.com.au).

Here is a summary of the gospel of salvation in Christ:

1

- **God is the loving ruler of the world.**
- **He made the world.**
- **He made us rulers of the world under him.**

> *Worthy are you, our Lord and God,*
> *to receive glory and honor and power,*
> *for you created all things,*
> *and by your will they existed and were created.* — Revelation 4:11

But is that the way it is now?

2

- **We all reject the ruler — God — by trying to run life our own way without him.**
- **But we fail to rule ourselves or society or the world.**

> *None is righteous, no, not one;*
> *no one understands;*
> *no one seeks for God.*
> *All have turned aside.* — Romans 3:10-12

What will God do about this rebellion?

3

- God won't let us rebel forever.
- God's punishment for rebellion is death and judgment.

It is appointed for man to die once, and after that comes judgment. — Hebrews 9:27

God's justice sounds hard, but . . .

4

- Because of his love, God sent his Son into the world, the man Jesus Christ.
- Jesus always lived under God's rule.
- Yet by dying in our place he took our punishment and brought forgiveness.

Christ also suffered once for sins, the righteous for the unrighteous, that he might bring us to God. — 1 Peter 3:18

But that's not all. . .

5

- God raised Jesus to life again as the ruler of the world.
- Jesus . . .
  - has conquered death,
  - now gives new life,
  - and will return to judge.

According to his great mercy, he has caused us to be born again to a living hope through the resurrection of Jesus Christ from the dead. —1 Peter 1:3

Well, where does that leave us?

6

THE TWO WAYS TO LIVE

OUR WAY:	GOD'S NEW WAY:
Reject the ruler — God	Submit to Jesus as our ruler
Try to run life our own way	Rely on Jesus's death and resurrection

RESULT:
Condemned by God
Facing death and judgment

RESULT:
Forgiven by God
Given eternal life

Whoever believes in the Son has eternal life; whoever does not obey the Son shall not see life, but the wrath of God remains on him.—John 3:36

Which of these represents the way you want to live?

MAKING A PRAYER NOTEBOOK

This section shares the structure of our prayer notebook. You will, of course, need to tailor this to your situation and need. The important thing is to do whatever we can to form a habit of prayer.

TEXTS FOR *MEDITATION* SECTION

The Ten Commandments
Exodus 20:1-17
The Beatitudes
Matthew 5:1-10
The fruit of the Spirit
Galatians 5:22-23
The necessity of a radical righteousness from heaven
Romans 1:16-17
Romans 3:21-26
Philippians 3:9
1 Corinthians 1:30
2 Corinthians 5:21

TEXTS FOR *CONFESSION* SECTION

Scriptures that instruct believers regarding their sinfulness and the necessity of confession.
Romans 3:9-18
Ephesians 2:1-3
Psalm 51:3-5
Psalm 139:23-24

TEXTS FOR *SUBMISSION* SECTION

Scriptures that illustrate or call for submission.

Isaiah 6:1-8
Proverbs 3:5-6
Romans 12:1-2
Matthew 11:28-30
This section also includes:
Prayers we have written submitting ourselves to God.
Prayers of submission written by others.

Texts for *Adoration* Section

Worship of God
Mark 14:1-9
John 4:23-24
Psalm 108:1
Exodus 33:11
Celebration of God's creatorship
Psalm 19:1-4
Psalm 29
Psalm 104
Job 26:7-14
Job 38:1-41
Colossians 1:15-20
John 1:1-3
1 Corinthians 8:6
Holiness of God
Isaiah 6:1-8
Exodus 19:16-19
Revelation 4:1-11
Devotion to God
In this section of the prayer notebook, we list forty selected psalms that express devotion. Our favorite is Psalm 63:1-7:

> *0 God, you are my God,*
> *earnestly I seek you;*
> *my soul thirsts for you;*
> *my flesh faints for you,*
> *as in a dry and weary land*
> *where there is no water.*

So I have looked upon you in the sanctuary,
beholding your power and glory.
Because your steadfast love is better than life,
my lips will praise you.
So I will bless you as long as I live;
in your name I will lift up my hands.
My soul will be satisfied as with fat and rich food,
and my mouth will praise you with joyful lips,
when I remember you upon my bed,
and meditate on you in the watches of the night;
for you have been my help,
and in the shadow of your wings I will sing for joy.

Hymns of Praise

We have compiled numerous hymns and songs that best express our hearts, some of which are:

"Fairest Lord Jesus"
"My Jesus, I Love Thee"
"Jesus, the Very Thought of Thee"
"When I Survey the Wondrous Cross"
"There Is a Redeemer"
"O Lord, You're Beautiful"

Poetry of Adoration

The Adoration section ends with poetry and readings that are especially meaningful to us. Here is a favorite, Gerard Manley Hopkins's "O Deus Ego Amo Te":

O God, I love Thee, I love Thee —
Not out of hope of heaven for me
Nor fearing not to love and be
In the everlasting burning.
Thou, Thou, my Jesus, after me
Didst reach Thine arms out dying,
For my sake sufferedst nails and lance,
Mocked and marred countenance,
Sorrows passing number
Sweat and care and cumber,
Yea and death, and this for me,

And Thou couldest see me sinning:
Then I, why should not I love Thee;
Jesus so much in love with me?
Not for heaven's sake; not to be
Out of hell by loving Thee;
Not for any gains I see;
But just that Thou didst me
I do and I will love Thee:
What must I love Thee, Lord, for then? —
For being my King and God. Amen.[1]

Common ~ sense Tips Regarding Discipline

How to Make Bedtime Pleasant and Avoid Bedlam

Tucking Them in

1. Make certain their beds are comfortable and clean.
2. Make sure they are clean, properly dressed for bed, and warm.
3. Don't rush them.
4. Read and pray with them.
5. Then say good night with a smile on your face.
6. Keep smiling as you close the door, cheerfully saying, "I'll see you in the morning."

After Tucking Them in

1. From the very beginning, *do not* let them get back up once they've been tucked in unless there is an emergency. If you give in, especially in response to screaming and crying, you will confirm the idea that they can control you if they fuss enough.
2. After your children have gone to sleep, slip back into their room and put a few small toys in their crib so that upon awaking in the morning, they'll have something to play with before you come to get them.
3. As they grow older, maintain the same routine, but instead of putting toys in the crib, occasionally slip a small surprise under their pillow.

How to Establish Good Eating Habits and Avoid Mealtime Madness

1. When your doctor says that it is time to begin serving solid foods and allows for some variety, *be sure that you continue to offer different tastes*. If

the baby doesn't like a certain food at first, don't give up. Always give him at least one bite. If you do this consistently, the baby will acquire a liking for *most* foods. Our observation is that often parents find it easier to give the baby what goes down with the least resistance, actually encouraging a limited range of foods that the child likes.

2. Keep up this one-bite practice, giving toddlers what our family came to call "no thank you helpings." If a child didn't like a particular food, he or she had to have at least a small helping, which eventually became a small spoon size rather than one bite. And they *had* to eat it. In this manner, our children acquired a taste for most foods. Dialogue hint: If your child objects, "I don't like it!" a helpful response is: "I don't ask that you like it, only that you eat it."

3. If you believe that you have already lost the battle here and have given up any hope of getting your child to eat what you place before him, *think again*. Remember that every time spoiled behavior is catered to, it will become a little worse. And this same willfulness will carry over into areas of far greater importance. Make up *your* mind that your child will eat his dinner. In carrying this out, refrain from using "if" threats: "If you don't eat this, you will sit here all day." Rather, decide on a plan and stick to it. You'll have some miserable mealtimes, but hang in there. Once he has to eat *one meal*, he'll begin to understand that you really mean business. You can do it!

4. If your child spills his milk, don't make a federal case out of it. Kids spill their drinks. They're clumsy. When our children were young, we had few meals when one of them didn't spill a drink. But there came a day when the last glass was knocked over, the last mess cleaned up, and we can't even remember when it was.

PUNISHMENT FOR WRONGDOING

1. Remember that the goal of discipline is not punishment but an inner conviction of what is right (Eph. 6:1).

2. Remember that your child needs you the most when he or she is defiant and difficult.

3. Remember, punishment should be equal to the offense. An action that might endanger his life or a moral offense such as lying or stealing will obviously necessitate a greater punishment than breaking a dish or coming home late from the next-door neighbor's house.

4. Remember that each child is unique. A sensitive child may shrink at a raised voice, while another, less sensitive, may be defiant even after a spanking.

5. A few words about spanking: We did! The Scriptures command it: "Foolishness is bound up in the heart of a child; the rod of discipline will remove it far from him" (Prov. 22:15, NASB). While this Scripture does not teach that *all* discipline is corporal, "the rod" has its proper use.

Of course, we did not spank our children for every infraction. Most offenses do not merit spanking. We also found that other disciplines were often more effective. (See "A Few Discipline Options" below.)

Common sense dictates that spanking ought to hurt — *some*. But all parents must understand that spanking is *not* a beating. Beating is child abuse. Spanking is a *brief, controlled, painful* punishment intended to make the recipient sorry he or she committed the offense that brought it about. Very often only a swat or two is necessary.

When administering such discipline, we gave the simple explanation, "What you did was wrong." We did not refrain from expressing our dismay or anger at the wrongdoing. But we always affirmed our love before and after the discipline. After all, godly discipline is an act of love. Similarly, punishment is not positively effective without a background of praise.

Many times we offered grace: "You deserve a spanking, but we're not going to give you one."

A regret regarding spanking: We once gave our eldest daughter a spanking, following the advice of an "expert" who advised to "spank until they cry softly." To this day she remembers that spanking as unjust, and she is right. Please, *keep spanking in perspective.*

A Few Discipline Options

1. *Removal of a privilege.* This is a very effective method of discipline but requires careful thought. A wise parent will not spontaneously blurt forth a restriction. Rather, if one is married, it should be discussed with the spouse. We have seen Christian parents take away privileges that were actually proving beneficial to their children. Long-range restrictions are generally unwise. If you discover that your restriction is unwise, explain that you have made a mistake, and remove the restriction.

2. *Sitting in a corner.* Of course, this is for young children and can be very effective for the child who always wants to be where the action is. When using it, remember that five minutes facing a corner can be an eternity for many children.

3. *Going to one's room.* Instructing your child to "Go to your room to think about it" will often give him time to cool off and reflect on his wrongdoing. The confinement is mildly disciplinary and often can lead to some reasonable discussion about the offense. Likewise, "Go to your room until you can come out pleasant" can be effective with an emotional or hot-tempered child as long as the device is not used by the parent to avoid discussing things. Remember to restrict, if applicable, the child's use of the phone, television, and video games. Some bedrooms are like Club Med. Again, be reasonable about the length of time the child remains in the room.

4. *Taking punishment in the child's place.* The great Christian educator Henrietta Mears told how her mother would sometimes deny herself the pleasure of butter at meals when Henrietta had been bad. This little technique had a chastening effect on the offending child. Common sense dictates, however, that such a method should be used sparingly and charitably.

A Few Things to Say When You Don't Know What to Say

1. "No!" This may be expressed as:
   "Absolutely not!"
   "Nothing doing!"
   "Cut it out!"
   "Enough is enough."
   "That will do."
   "Arguing will get you nowhere."
   "STOP IT!"

All of the above are common-sense expressions that parents have used for ages. It's OK to say these things — just let your children know you have every intention of standing behind these words.

2. "No, you may not, but you may do one of these three things . . . Which one do you choose?" (This diffuses the deprived, "poor me" feeling.)

3. "I can't allow you to talk like that to me because of what it will do to *you*!" (This is for the sweet young thing who overnight turned into a smart-aleck adolescent.)

4. "You're a great kid, but you're *acting* like an undisciplined brat — STOP IT!" (Ditto.)

5. "You *will* obey, with or without punishment; it's your choice." This is for the child who says, "I won't do it!" Calmly explain that he (or she) most certainly will do it, and the only options he has are to do it immediately without punishment or to try delaying, in which case he will *still* obey, *with* punishment.

6. If a child is misbehaving at the dinner table, and guests are present, say something like, "John, please come help me in the kitchen." This allows him to save face and provides the privacy to give a word of instruction.

SUGGESTED READING LISTS
FOR CHILDREN

☙

Next to my computer is a poster with several quotes about reading. My favorite is by William Faulkner: "Read, read, read. Read everything. . . ." That's good advice, especially for children. Let them read the newspaper, the back of the cereal box, the road atlas, and even billboards.

As parents, however, you probably would like a little more guidance than merely letting your children read everything. First of all, a cautionary piece of advice. If a writer is promoting a cause, chances are he or she isn't telling a story, even if the cause is Christian. Good stories come from human experience. In *The Spying Heart* (a book about reading and writing for children), Newberry award-winning children's author Katherine Paterson describes her job: "My job is to tell a story — a story about real people who live in the world as it is."

When you read a good book, you might not always agree with the writer's view of life, and you might not get a happily-ever-after ending. But when you have finished the book, you'll understand a little bit more about life and people. That's what makes a satisfying book.

Wait a minute! Aren't we talking about children's books? You know, talking animals and cute pictures. Fortunately, there's a lot more to kids' books than "cute." Children's books, like adult books, have specific characters (be they animal, vegetable, or human) who confront conflict (cosmic or personal) and grow as a result of facing that conflict. In other words, they have all the elements of a good story: character, conflict, and resolution.

Good children's literature will also handle sensitive issues in a sensitive way. Even though your first inclination might be to avoid all books about death and dying, a book such as *Bridge to Teribethea* by Katherine Paterson could also open the way for conversations about death, eternal life, and heaven —those big, important issues. By the way, *Bridge to Teribethea* was based on a real experience that happened to Paterson's nine-year-old son. Her book was a mother's way of helping her son cope with his grief over a playmate's death.

While some books might be more appropriate for some ages than others, let your children guide themselves. True, you need to exercise control over their choices, but you might be surprised at what your kids actually enjoy reading — with or without parental influence. One more piece of advice from Paterson: Choose the stories you loved as a kid for your kids to read. The fringe benefit in this piece of advice is that you'll have a chance to get reacquainted with some old friends.

In general, children's books are classified into these categories: picture books, young readers, intermediate readers, and young adult.

Picture books (or read-aloud books) are just that — books with big, colorful, fun illustrations and a few sentences on each page. Start looking at picture books with your kids as soon as you can. How soon is soon? When a friend's daughter was just six months old, Grandfather read the little one the Latin classics — in the original language no less! Of course, Grandpa was a Latin professor, but you get the idea.

Books for young readers, usually ages six to eight, are still heavy on the pictures, but there's more copy, the characters are developed a little more, and there's even conflict and resolution. Actually, many of the young reader books are funny, especially for the adults in the house.

When you think of your favorite childhood books, chances are that most of your choices would fall into the intermediate category. Once your kids graduate to these books, usually ages nine to twelve, they're ready to read on their own as well as choose their own books. These books might have an illustration or two, but the characters, plot, conflict, and resolution are as well defined as in any adult novel. (And you can throw out that crazy notion that *anyone* can write children's books. It takes just as much skill and talent as all those grown-up writers have to write good books for kids.)

This appendix was compiled by a committee of mothers and their children. No list can be foolproof for everyone because people's tastes vary, as do the developmental levels of children. Items on the following lists that are preceded by an ★ indicate authors or books particularly affirmed among the people who compiled the list. Some authors or titles are followed by cautions, but the need for parental involvement actually extends to all books that children read. Not included are important categories such as biographies and sports books for boys.

BOOKS ABOUT CHILDREN'S LITERATURE

Vigen Guroian, *Tending the Heart: How Classic Stories Awaken a Child's Moral Imagination* (not a book of lists, but a book that will allow parents to guide and nurture a child's reading with increased understanding of the dynamics of the process).

Gladys Hunt, *Honey for a Child's Heart* (updated version if possible) and *Read for Your Life: Turning Teens Into Readers.*

Kathryn Lindskoog and Ranelda Mack Hunsicker, *How to Grow a Young Reader: Books from Every Age for Readers of Every Age.*

Jim Trelease, *New Revised Read Aloud Handbook.*

Elizabeth Wilson, *Books Children Love: A Guide to the Best Children's Literature.*

PICTURE BOOKS (AUTHORS ONLY)

★Allan and Janet Ahlberg
Aliki
John Archambault
★Alan Baker
Jill Barton
★Stan and Jan Berenstain
Emilie Boon
Franz Brandenberg
★Margaret Wise Brown
Anthony Browne
John Burningham

★Jez Alborough
★M. M. Anno
Frank Asch
Byron Barton
Ludwig Bemelmens
Barbara Berger
★Sandra Boynton
★Jan Brett
Mark Brown
Eve Bunting
Virginia Lee Burton

PICTURE BOOKS (AUTHORS ONLY) CONTINUED

Mary Calhoun
Nancy White Carlstrom
Barbara Cooney
*Alexandra Day
Tomie DePaola

*Dr. Seuss

Elizabeth George
Mirra Ginsburg
Eric Hill
Jane Hissy
Tana Hoban
Shirley Hughes
Pat Hutchins
Rachel Isadora
*Ezra Jack Keats
Steven Kellogg
*Kim Lewis
Anita Lobel
James Marshall
Sam McBratney
David McKee
David McPhail
Laura Numeroff
*Helen Oxenbury
*Watty Piper
*H. A. and Margaret Rey
*Anne and Harlow Rockwell
*Michel Rosen
*Richard Scarry
Shel Silverstein
William Steig
Robert Louis Stevenson

*Eric Carle
Judith Casely
Donald Crews
Jean De Brunhoff
*Dorling Kindersley (publisher)
    Eyewitness series
    See How They Grow series
*Lois Ehlert
    Eye Opener series
Gail Gibbons
Kevin Henkes
Anna Grossnickle Hines
*Russell Hoban
Katharine Holabird
Angela Elwell Hunt
*Mick Inkpen
Ann Jonas
Holly Keller
Jill Krementz
*Maj Lindman
*Arnold Lobel
*Bill Martin, Jr.
*Robert McCloskey
Bruce McMillan
Jill Murphy
Jan Ormerod
Bill Peet
Maria Polushkin
Eve Rice
Fred Rogers
*Cynthia Rylant
Nancy Shaw
*Peter Speir
James Stevenson
Cyndy Szekeres

Jeanne Titherington
*Janice May Udry
Bernard Weber
Rosemary Wells
Ian Whybrow

*Eliose Wilkin
*Audrey Wood
Arthur Yorinks
*Charolotte Zolotow

*Rasha Tudor
*Martin and Barbara Firth Waddell
Nicki Weiss
Nadine Bernard Westcott
Walter Wick and Jean Marzollo
   Eye Spy series
Vera Williams
Jane Yolen
Harriet Ziefert

YOUNG READERS (INCLUDING READ-ALOUD AND EMERGING READERS)

*David A. Adler, *Cam Jansen Mystery*
*American Girl Series
*Richard Atwater, *Mr. Popper's Penguins*
Frans Bischer, *Jimmy Dale*
*Michael Bond, Paddington series
*Walter R. Brooks, The Freddy Collection series
*Childhood of Young Americans series
*Beverly Cleary, *Henry Huggins* and numerous others
Anne Colver, *Bread and Butter Indian*
Scott Corbett, *The Lemonade Trick*
*Alice Dalgliesh, *The Courage of Sarah Noble*
*Paula Danziger, *Amber Brown*
*Franklin W. Dixon, Hardy Boys series
*Clancy Holling, *Paddle to the Sea* and others
*Carolyn Keene, Nancy Drew series
*Robert Lawson, *Ben and Me* and *Rabbit Hill*
*Peter Leithart, *Wise Words* (based on Proverbs)
*Arnold Lobel, *Frog and Toad*
*Betty MacDonald, *Mrs. Piggle Wiggle* and sequels
*Patricia MacLachlan, *Sarah, Plain and Tall* and others
*Robert McCloskey, *Homer Price*
*James Marshall, *George and Martha*
*A. A. Milne, *Winnie the Pooh* and others

YOUNG READERS (INCLUDING READ-ALOUD AND EMERGING READERS) CONTINUED

*Else Holmelund Minarik, *Little Bear*
*Mary Nash, *While Mrs. Coverlet Was Away*
*Zora Louise Olsen, *Herman the Great*
*Mary Pope Osborn, *Magic Tree House*
*Mary Pope Park, *Junie B. Jones*
*Peggy Parrish, *Amelia Bedelia*
Katherine Paterson, *Angels and Other Strangers* (Christmas collection)
*John Peterson, *The Littles*
*Beatrix Potter, *The Tale of Peter Rabbit* and others
*Barbara Robinson, *The Best Christmas Pageant Ever*
Thomas Rockwell, *How to Eat Fried Worms*
*Cynthia Rylant, *Henry and Mudge*
*George Seldon, *The Cricket in Times Square* and sequels
*Marjorie Weinman Sharmat, *Nate the Great*
*Donald J. Sobol, *Encyclopedia Brown*
Gertrude Chandler Warner, *The Boxcar Children*
Jerry West, The Happy Hollisters series
*E. B. White, *Charolotte's Web, Stuart Little,* and *The Trumpet of the Swan*
*Laura Ingalls Wilder, Little House series

INTERMEDIATE READERS

*Louisa May Alcott, *Little Women* and others
Lloyd Alexander, Prydain Chronicles series, The Vesper Holly Adventures series, and The Westmark series
William H. Armstrong, *Sounder*
Joan W. Blos, *A Gathering of Days*
*Frances Hodgson Burnett, *The Secret Garden* and *Little Princess*
*Sheila Burnford, *The Incredible Journey*
*Mary Calhoun, *Katie John* and sequels
Roald Dahl, *The BFG* and others
*Marguerite de Angeli, historical fiction
*Meindert De Jong, *The Wheel on the School*
*Henry Dennis, *King of the Wind*
*Mary Mapes Dodge, *Hans Brinker and the Silver Skates*

⋆William Penn DuBois, *Twenty-one Balloons*

⋆Walter Farley, *The Black Stallion* and sequels

⋆Dorothy Canfield Fisher, *Understood Betsy*

⋆Sid Fleischman, *By the Great Horn Spoon*

⋆Esther Forbes, *Johnny Tremain*

⋆Jean Fritz, various nonfiction

John Gardiner, *Stone Fox*

Jean Craighead George, *My Side of the Mountain* and sequels

⋆Kenneth Grahame, *The Wind in the Willows*

⋆Roger Lancelyn Green, *Robin Hood* and *King Arthur*

⋆Marguerite Henry, Misty of Chincoteaque series and others

Karen Hesse, *Stowaway*

⋆Ryle Howard, *Otto of the Silver Hand*

⋆Norman Hunter, Professor Branestawm series

⋆Brian Jacques, Redwall series

⋆Norton Juster, *Phantom Tollbooth*

⋆E. L. Konigsburg, *From the Mixed-up Files of Mrs. Basil E. Frankweiler, The View from Saturday*, and others

Janet Lambert, Penny Parrish series

⋆Jean Lee Latham, *Carry on, Mr. Bowditch*

⋆Lois Lenski, *Indian Captive*

⋆C. S. Lewis, The Chronicles of Narnia series

⋆Astrid Lindgren, *Pippi Longstocking* and sequels

Betty Bao Lord, *In the Year of the Boar* and *Jackie Robinson*

⋆Maud Hart Lovelace, Betsy Tacey series

⋆Lois Lowry, *Number the Stars*

Jean Merrill, *The Pushcart War*

⋆E. Nesbit, The Bastable Children series, *The Railway Children, Five Children and It*, and others

Sterling North, *Rascal*

⋆Robert C. O'Brien, *Mrs. Frisby and the Rats of Nimh*

⋆Wilson Rawls, *Where the Red Fern Grows*

⋆Anna Sewell, *Black Beauty*

Margery Sharp, The Rescuers series

⋆Eric Sloane, *Diary of an Early American Boy*

⋆Patricia St. John, *Treasures in the Snow* and others

⋆Noel Streatfeild, *Ballet Shoes* and others

Intermediate Readers continued

*Sidney Taylor, All-of-a-Kind Family series
Mark Twain, *Tom Sawyer* and *Huckleberry Finn*
John White, The Tower of Geburah series
*Elizabeth Winthrop, *The Castle in the Attic*
*Elizabeth Yates, *Amos Fortune, Free Man*

Young Adult Readers

American Diaries series, especially the ones dealing with immigrants
Avi, *Crispin* and others
Natalie Babbitt, *Tuck Everlasting* and *Search for Delicious*
*Thyra Ferre Bjorn, *Papa's Wife* and others
*Douglas Bond, *Duncan's War*, from the still emerging Crown and
Covenant series
Nancy Bond, *A Place to Come Back to* and others
Anthony Buckeridge, Jennings series
*Lewis Carroll, *Alice in Wonderland*
Sook Nyui Choi, *Year of Impossible Good-byes* and others
John Christopher, Pool of Fire series
James and Christopher Collier, *Who Is Carrie?* and others
Sharon Creech, *Walk Two Moons*
Karen Cushman, *Catherine, Called Birdy*, and others
Ingri D'Aulaire and Edgar Parin, *Book of Greek Myths*
*Harold Deith, *Rifles for Waite*
*George Eliot, *Silas Marner*
Paul Fleishman, *Bull Run* and others
Paula Fox, *One-Eyed Cat* and *Monkey Island*
Anne Frank, *Diary of a Young Girl* (parental discretion required)
*Benedict and Nancy Freedman, *Mrs. Mike*
*Frank B. Gilbreth, Jr., *Cheaper by the Dozen* and others
*Frederick Gipson, *Old Yeller*
Elizabeth Goudge, many titles
*Elizabeth Gray, *Adam of the Road*
*Kristiana Gregory, *Earthquake at Dawn*
Margaret Peterson Haddix, Among the Hidden series
Virginia Hamilton, *The House of Dies Drear*

*Sally Heehn, *I am Regina* (parental discretion required)
*Karen Hesse, *Phoenix Rising* and *Out of the Dust*
*James Herriot, *All Creatures Great and Small* and sequels
Will Hobbes, various adventure series
*Irene Hunt, *Up a Road Slowly* and *Across Five Aprils*
*Eric P. Kelly, *The Trumpeter of Krakow*
Ursula LeGuin, multiple titles
*Madeleine L'Engle, Murry Family series, O'Keefe Family series, Austin Family series, and others. The early L'Engle is more reliable than the later L'Engle; parents should read the later books to determine if they approve of them.

Jack London, *Call of the Wild*
*George MacDonald, *The Princess and Curdie, The Princess and the Goblins, At the Back of the North Wind*
Robin McKinley, *The Blue Sword* and others
*Catherine Marshall, *Christy* and *Julie*
*L. M. Montgomery, *Anne of Green Gables* and sequels
Ralph Moody, *Little Britches*
*Walter Morey, *Gentle Ben*
Scott O'Dell, *Alexandra* and others
*Katherine Paterson, *Angels and Other Strangers* (Christmas collection), *Jacob Have I Loved*, and others
*Arthur Ransome, Swallows and Amazons series
Ellen Raskin, *The Westing Game*
Wilson Rawls, *Summer of the Monkeys*
Carolyn Reeder, *Shades of Gray*
Anne Rinaldi, historical fiction
Louis Sacchar, *Holes*
Ouida Sebestyn, *Words by Heart*
*Kate Seredy, *Good Master, The Singing Tree*, and others
Dava Sobel, *Longitude*
Elizabeth George Speare, *The Bronze Bow* and *The Sign of the Beaver*
Jerry Spinelli, *Mania Magee*
Robert Louis Stevenson, *Kidnapped* and *Treasure Island*
*Mildred D. Taylor, *Roll of Thunder, Hear My Cry* and sequels, *The Friendship*, and *The Gold Cadillac*
*Corrie ten Boom, *The Hiding Place* (Holocaust realism)

YOUNG ADULT READERS CONTINUED

Bodie Thoene, Zion Covenant series, Zion Chronicle series (parental discretion advised in selection of individual books)

⋆J. R. R. Tolkien, *The Hobbit* and The Lord of the Rings series

⋆James Ramsey Ullman, *Banner in the Sky*

Jean Webster, *Daddy Longlegs*

James C. Whittaker, *We Thought We Heard Angels Sing*

Patricia Wrede, Dealing with Dragons series

Lawrence Yep, *Dragon's Gate*, *Dragonwings*, and others

Jane Yolen, *The Devil's Arithmetic* (Holocaust material)

Suggestions for Assembling a Home Video Library

CLASSICS

Rebecca
Mr. Smith Goes to Washington
It Happened One Night
Mr. Deeds Goes to Town
Laura
How Green Was My Valley
A Christmas Carol
Friendly Persuasion
Bridge on the River Kwai
Ben Hur
A Man for All Seasons
North by Northwest

AMERICAN FILMS

To Kill a Mockingbird
The Trip to Bountiful
Tender Mercies
Glory
Sounder
Where the Red Fern Grows
Fiddler on the Roof
The Black Stallion
To Sleep with Anger
Anne of Green Gables
A Cry in the Dark

SUPPLEMENTAL VIDEO LIST

The following material appeared in *World Magazine* (June 28, 2003) and is reprinted by permission (www.worldmag.com).

Moonlight Movies

Fifty recommended films that can be a vibrant and useful part of family life
    By Andrew Coffin

Since we must rest and play, where can we do so better than here — in the suburbs of Jerusalem? It is lawful to rest our eyes in the moonlight — especially [since] we know where it comes from, that it is only sunlight at second hand.

C. S. Lewis didn't have movies specifically in mind when he put down these words in his classic essay on "Christianity and Culture," but his words well describe the collection of films contained below. Some movies are harmful, but good movies are second-hand sunlight, and to the discerning viewer — to the discerning family — they can be a vibrant and useful part of family life.

Containing some easy films and some more challenging (Lewis also said that "a little sense of labour is necessary to all perfect pleasures"), this list is designed to help families dig deeper in the vast film canon of the past 100 years. It attempts to reflect an emphasis on overall quality rather than the simple absence of offensive elements or presence of positive themes.

This list ignores two important categories: films aimed for the youngest children (say 3 and under), and films aimed at adults that may be deemed suitable for older kids (R-rated films such as *Schindler's List*). It favors movies with broad appeal, but recognizes that families with elementary-school children will look for different films than families with high-school-age kids. So the list is broken into three categories: 15 films for young children, 15 films more appropriate for older kids, and 20 films that we hope will split the difference.

This is by no means a list of the 50 best movies of all time, although many of these films would be serious contenders for that distinction. It is, however, a group of films selected because they will delight most viewers and show a pale reflection of the sunlight that is capable of challenging our minds, softening our hearts, bolstering our courage . . . and yes, entertaining us along the way to Jerusalem.

Note: Film titles are followed by the year of release and director; films released or re-released after 1968 include MPAA ratings. Parents have a wide variety of standards and should preview films and be ready with fast-forward buttons. Some movies are objectionable in theater versions but are more likely to meet parental standards when edited for television.

Families with Younger Children

The Little Colonel (1935/David Butler) A Shirley Temple classic in which a little girl mends the relationship between her mother and grandfather in the post-Civil War South. Includes the famous stair-dancing sequence with Bill Robinson.

Snow White and the Seven Dwarves (1937/David Hand) and **Pinocchio** (1940/Hamilton Luske & Ben Sharpsteen) Great songs, dazzling (and groundbreaking) animation, and endlessly colorful supporting characters make these two early Disney cartoons timeless, ageless classics.

The Wizard of Oz (1939/G/Victor Fleming) When it was released, *Oz* was advertised as "The Biggest Screen Sensation Since Snow White," and it still lives up to that boast, despite advances in technology. Frank Baum's story is a fantasy classic that gently communicates real-world lessons.

National Velvet (1944/G/Clarence Brown) Young Mickey Rooney and Elizabeth Taylor shine in a horse movie with great steeplechase races and a "follow your dreams" theme that still doesn't seem as clichéd as that sentiment now sounds.

The Yearling (1946/G/Clarence Brown) One of the greatest father-son relationships ever put on film. A farmer (Gregory Peck) struggles in post-Civil War Florida, where his son's eyes are opened to the harsh realities of life through his love for a motherless fawn.

Pollyanna and **The Parent Trap** (1960 and 1961/G/David Swift) Two Hayley Mills classics that prove that Disney was still making good movies in the '60s. The admittedly incomplete worldview of Pollyanna is unjustly reviled today.

Swiss Family Robinson (1960/G/Ken Annakin) A great family adventure that bears little resemblance to the story on which it's based, but is nonetheless an imaginative tale of a shipwrecked family's survival on a deserted tropical island.

Mary Poppins (1964/G/Robert Stevenson) It's not easy imagining a live-action Disney film today matching the five Oscars that this classic deservedly won. It's just as hard imagining a film today that has this much fun teaching kids to respect their parents.

The Sound of Music (1965/G/Robert Wise) Julie Andrews in an

Oscar-winning musical that has claimed the hearts of generations, with grand songs, an affecting love story, and an exciting World War II subplot.

The Black Stallion (1979/G/Carroll Ballard) A tragic shipwreck bonds a young boy and the mysterious horse aboard the same vessel in a story helped immeasurably by its glorious cinematography.

Annie (1982/PG/John Huston) The Broadway musical was brought to over-the-top life on-screen by Albert Finney, Carol Burnett, Tim Curry, and a charismatic performance by Aileen Quinn as the title character.

Babe (1995/G/Chris Noonan) A mix of real animals, mechanical doubles, and computer animation creates a barnyard of talking live-stock—and the surprise is that what they have to say will delight both children and their parents.

Toy Story and *Toy Story 2* (1995 and 1999/G/John Lasseter) Two of the few truly grand films Disney has produced since its early heyday, the Toy Story movies contain a near-perfect mix of humor, adventure, feeling, and technical wizardry.

Chicken Run (2000/G/Peter Lord and Nick Park) Spectacular *Great Escape*-style adventure, only this time it's claymation hens trying to make the break for freedom. If you enjoy this inventive feature, check out Mr. Park's even better "Wallace and Grommet" shorts.

Spy Kids (2001/PG/Robert Rodriguez) *Spy Kids* is one of the few concessions on this list to the high-speed, special-effects-driven entertainment that defines modern children's movies. In this case, however, the story is just as gleefully inventive as the gadgets and gizmos that spice it up.

Other good ones include *Aladdin*, *The Fox and the Hound*, *Stuart Little*, *Darby O'Gill and the Little People*, *The Little Princess*, *The Secret Garden*, *Heidi*, *A Bug's Life*, *Davy Crockett*, *The Absent-Minded Professor*, and *Monsters, Inc.*

The Middle Ground

Bringing Up Baby (1938/Howard Hawks) *Baby* is a great entry point into the screwball comedies of the '30s, with Cary Grant and Katharine Hepburn in top form as a zoologist and an heiress, respectively.

Mr. Smith Goes to Washington (1939/Frank Capra) Jimmy Stewart plays the earnest young Jefferson Smith, appointed to the U.S. Senate to fill a vacant seat. Idealism crashes head-on into deep-seated corruption. Guess which — thankfully — wins out?

Sergeant York (1941/Howard Hawks) This is the true story of Alvin C. York, one of the most celebrated heroes of World War I and a onetime conscientious objector. York's conversion and struggle to understand his new faith in light of the looming war is among the best presentations of Christianity ever put on film. A thrilling story with endless possibilities for family discussions.

It's a Wonderful Life (1946/Frank Capra) Another Christmas classic that does in fact improve with repeated viewings. The religious element is hokey, but the sentiments are pure and never fail to tug at the heart.

High Noon (1952/Fred Zinnemann) This "real time" countdown to a showdown between the town sheriff (Gary Cooper) and some really bad men is thrilling as a Western and profound as a picture of a crisis of conscience.

Singin' in the Rain (1952/Stanley Donen) Probably the best movie musical ever made, this film is also a behind-the-scenes look at the sometimes painful transition from silence to sound in 1927 Hollywood.

Shane (1953/George Stevens) A complex Western that challenges viewers on many levels, as a loner makes the difficult decision to defend a family from the powerful cattleman gunning for its land.

The Man Who Knew Too Much (1956/PG/Alfred Hitchcock) Not the best of Hitchcock's thrillers by any means, *Man* is still an easily accessible entry point for younger viewers learning to appreciate the Master of Suspense, on the way to more mature fare like *Vertigo* and *Rear Window*.

Charade (1963/Stanley Donen) With humor too adult and villains too scary for younger kids, *Charade* is still a thoroughly entertaining ride for much of the family, with Cary Grant and Audrey Hepburn generating the perfect mix of sharp-witted humor and Hitchcockian suspense.

The Star Wars trilogy (1977, 1980, 1983/PG/George Lucas, Irvin Kershner, and Richard Marquand) Mr. Lucas's recent additions to the series may not have lived up to the promise of the first three films, but that shouldn't diminish the power of this modern myth narrative. Families can discuss the way the films' struggle between good and evil relates to — and does not relate to — a biblical understanding.

Chariots of Fire (1981/PG/Hugh Hudson) Beloved by many as a "Christian" classic, this story is more complex than that label implies.

Eric Liddell's courage and conviction do shine wonderfully through this chronicle of runners in the 1924 Olympics, though. The example of his faith makes the film worth showing to younger children who may not yet "get" the rest of the story.

E.T. the Extra-Terrestrial (1982/PG/Steven Spielberg) Mr. Spielberg's remarkable ability to tell a story to which people of all ages connect has never been more evident than in this tale of a visitor from outer space. A B-grade story that shouldn't have worked is instead transformed into what was — and is — for many a defining movie-going experience.

The Man from Snowy River (1982/PG/George Miller) This Australian Western is straightforward family fun, family drama, forbidden love, the journey to manhood, rapturous scenery, and some of the most remarkable riding you'll ever see on film.

A Christmas Carol (1984/Clive Donner) An excellent British cast headed by a never-better George C. Scott makes this TV movie of the Dickens classic a commendable Christmas tradition.

The Princess Bride (1987/PG/Rob Reiner) A few coarse elements are the only blight on this very funny fairy tale that manages to simultaneously spoof and re-enliven the genre. Inconceivable.

White Fang (1991/PG/Randal Kleiser) Another Disney entry that expands on the theme of a classic tale, rather than straightforwardly adapting it. Good performances, beautiful scenery, and solid storytelling help make this story of a boy and his dog work on all levels, however.

Into the West (1992/PG/Mike Newell) and *The Secret of Roan Inish* (1994/PG/John Sayles) Two Irish fables made by talented filmmakers of typically more adult films, joined by a common (sometimes dark) mood, a deep appreciation for the power of myths, and an emphasis on the bonds of family.

Rudy (1993/PG/David Anspaugh) This movie mirrors its protagonist, overcoming seemingly insurmountable odds to become, respectively, a sports movie classic and the smallest, most unathletic player to make Notre Dame's football squad.

The Winslow Boy (1999/G/David Mamet) Remarkable simply for the fact that Mr. Mamet directed a G-rated film, *Boy* stands out in its own right as an examination of honor and family, set in the context of 1910 England.

The Rookie (2002/G/John Lee Hancock) Dennis Quaid gives a winning performance as baseball's oldest rookie.

Other good ones include *Harvey, White Christmas, That Thing You Do, Night Crossing, Arsenic and Old Lace, Father of the Bride, 20,000 Leagues Under the Sea, My Fair Lady, How the West Was Won, Gunga Din, The Adventures of Robin Hood, Hoosiers,* and *What's Up, Doc?*

Families with Older Children

Casablanca (1942/G/Michael Curtiz) A regular challenger to *Citizen Kane* at the top of "best" lists everywhere, with good reason. The remarkable ending may shock younger viewers who expect everything out of Hollywood to follow the same romantic formula.

Hamlet (1948, 1990, 1996/Unrated, PG, PG-13/Laurence Olivier, Franco Zeffirelli, Kenneth Branagh) Pick any one of the three most prominent adaptations of Shakespeare's most famous play — Olivier's definitive treatment, the very accessible Mel Gibson version, or Mr. Branagh's perhaps too complete translation to the screen. In all three the power of the bard's words and the complexity of his characters shine brilliantly through.

Key Largo (1948/John Huston) and *To Have and Have Not* (1944/Howard Hawks) Two Humphrey Bogart classics that are full of oft quoted lines and memorable scenes. It's hard to believe that potboilers were once made with this much class and character depth.

The Bridge on the River Kwai (1957/PG/David Lean) British and American soldiers struggle to maintain sanity and perspective in a Japanese prisoner of war camp during World War II. Equal parts action, adventure and psychological drama.

To Kill a Mockingbird (1962/Robert Mulligan) A southern black man is accused of rape, and the contentious trial is seen through the eyes of his defense attorney's (Gregory Peck) children. Searing, intelligent, and powerful.

The Great Escape (1963/John Sturges) This tale of Allied prisoners of war in a World War II German prison camp provides great characters, suspenseful action, never-give-up attitudes, and humor.

A Man for All Seasons (1966/G/Fred Zinnemann) A six-time Oscar winner about Sir Thomas More's conflict with King Henry VIII over the formation of the Church of England. Paul Scofield's More stands shoulder-to-shoulder with Liddell and York (see above) for great portrayals of faith on screen.

Gallipoli and *The Truman Show* (1981 and 1998/PG/Peter Weir) Two films that serve as crowning achievements in director Peter Weir's notable career, which is built around the careful examination of serious themes. The first tells the simple and heartbreaking story of two Australian sprinters sent to fight in the bloody title battle during World War I; the second features Jim Carrey in his best performance to date in a story that now seems eerily prescient, arriving before the boom of reality TV.

The Right Stuff (1983/PG/Philip Kaufman) A soaring film set at the beginning of the space era that ranks character and courageous accomplishment above the pursuit of fame and fortune, and depicts "the American character" perhaps better than any other film.

Henry V (1989/PG-13/Kenneth Branagh) Never before has Shakespeare been brought so vividly to life on screen. The rousing St. Crispin's Day speech will not fail to invigorate young minds.

Indiana Jones and the Last Crusade (1989/PG-13/Steven Spielberg) The final episode of the Indiana Jones trilogy, with lots of action and humor, and fewer of the elements that some parents find objectionable.

King of the Hill (1993/PG-13/Steven Soderbergh) Despite the presence of younger kids in the plot, this tale of Depression-era survival is for older children only. Mr. Soderbergh vividly films this period story, and its sometimes difficult themes will require a thoughtful debriefing.

Apollo 13 (1995/PG/Ron Howard) The breathtaking, true story of the nearly disastrous Apollo 13 space mission in 1970, which required the heroic efforts of both the air and ground crews to return the ship safely. Very few films achieve this level of excitement without featuring any violence.

Sense and Sensibility (1995/PG/Ang Lee) The title personality dichotomy, between two very different sisters, helps to illustrate the deeper themes almost always present in Jane Austen's writing: honor, integrity, and self-sacrificing love. It's also rapturously filmed by Mr. Lee and scripted with an excess of wit by Emma Thompson.

The Lord of the Rings trilogy (2001, 2002, and 2003/PG-13/Peter Jackson) If the yet-to-be-released third film in the trilogy matches the quality of the first two, Mr. Jackson's efforts will have produced one of the greatest film fantasies of all time. Despite running times requiring significant pruning of the original material, J.R.R. Tolkien's elaborate vision comes through with spirit — and many details — wonderfully intact.

Other good ones include *The Enemy Below, The Man Who Would Be King, The Hunt for Red October, The Guns of Navarone, Much Ado About Nothing, Cold Comfort Farm, Sleepless in Seattle, While You Were Sleeping, Quiz Show, Babette's Feast, The Hudsucker Proxy, Groundhog Day, The Man Who Shot Liberty Valance, Spider-man, Superman, Twelve Angry Men, Field of Dreams,* and *The Fugitive.*

VACATION SPOTS AND THEIR HISTORICAL OR LITERARY CONNECTIONS

❧

For a trip to California, you might want to read some of the short stories of California's venerable nineteenth-century authors such as Bret Harte's "The Outcasts of Poker Flat" or "The Luck of Roaring Camp" or Mark Twain's "The Celebrated Jumping Frog of Calaveras County" or Ambrose Bierce's "The Secret of Marcarger's Gulch."

Perhaps you would like to plan a vacation in the New England area. If so, an enriching approach would be to take a couple of days to dip into "literary New England," visiting the homes of famous authors while reading excerpts from their works. The homes of Henry David Thoreau, Ralph Waldo Emerson, Nathaniel Hawthorne, and Louisa May Alcott are all in Concord, Massachusetts (Emerson and Hawthorne, the same home). In nearby Cambridge are the homes of Henry Wadsworth Longfellow and Oliver Wendell Holmes and other Harvard literati. Interestingly, the historic homes of Mark Twain and Harriet Beecher Stowe (two opposites indeed!) are next to each other in Hartford, Connecticut.

Doing the Rockies and the surrounding West? Read Irving Stone's best-seller *Men to Match My Mountains,* and bring along a couple of Louis L'Amour's novels for the kids. Are your girls avid readers of the Anne of Green Gables series? You can include a trip to Prince Edward Island to accommodate that passion.

There are more literary sites than most people are aware of. A Midwestern edition of a recent AAA magazine carried an article entitled "Discover Their Roots," which gave information about Midwestern sites associated with Sherwood Anderson, Carl Sandburg, Willa Cather, Laura Ingalls Wilder, and Langston Hughes.

In this day of Internet search engines, you can almost certainly include visits to literary sites on your family vacations.

"FIRST HEARTBEAT"

I'm living inside this nice warm place.
I don't know my name but I feel warm and safe,
I've found my thumb and I hear her heartbeat.
Is she thinking of a kid like me?

Chorus: If the stars are numbered one by one
and He knows when we slumber
and when life's begun,
And he looks deep inside this heart of mine,
Then God knows about the first heartbeat.
Oh, God knows about the first heartbeat.

I can move from side to side,
I hear my mom's laughter, I know when she cries
She sings me sweet songs and lullabies.
Now it's time to say good night.

Chorus: If the stars are numbered one by one
and He knows when we slumber
and when life's begun,
And he looks deep inside this heart of mine,
Then God knows about the first heartbeat.
                    — Mary Rice Hopkins

SELECTED
HUGHES FAMILY RECIPES

The following favorites are by no means *haute cuisine* or calorie and cholesterol counting *(yes!)*, but basic, tried-and-true everyday cooking, which we hope will encourage you not to forsake the joys of the family table.

NO-FAIL CRESCENT ROLLS

1 pkg. dry yeast
4 C. flour, sifted
1 C. lukewarm milk
1 t. salt

½ C. sugar
½ C. butter, melted
2 eggs, well beaten

Mix yeast, flour, and milk. Let stand at room temperature for half an hour. Add remaining ingredients, stirring everything together in large bowl. Let stand overnight covered with a light cloth, without refrigeration.

Next day, divide into thirds. Roll into three circles, cutting each into eight pie-shaped pieces. Roll up, starting with wide end.

Place on greased cookie sheets and cover with a light cloth. Let rise for six hours. Bake at 400° for about 7 minutes. Serve hot with dinner.

Makes 24 rolls.

GREAT BAKING POWDER BISCUITS

Sift together three times:

2¼ C. flour	3 t. baking powder
½ t. salt	2 t. sugar
½ t. cream of tartar	

Cream in:

½ C. shortening	⅔ C. milk

Knead dough lightly on a floured pastry board or counter. Flatten out dough (with hand or rolling pin) to about ¾ inch, and cut out biscuits with cutter (or an upside-down drinking glass).

Place on greased cookie sheet and bake at 375° for 8-10 minutes. Makes 8-10 biscuits.

CRAZY CHOCOLATE CAKE

This is a great recipe for the children to make on their own.

Heat oven to 350°. Sift the following ingredients together two to three times directly into a 9-by-13-inch cake pan:

3 C. flour	2 t. baking soda
2 C. sugar	1 t. salt
6-8 T. baking cocoa	

Make three depressions in this mixture, and put one of the following into each:

¾ C. vegetable oil	2 t. vanilla
2 T. white vinegar	

Pour 2 cups cold water over all, and blend thoroughly with a fork. Pour one 8-ounce bag of chocolate chips (and 1/2 cup nuts, if desired) over batter.

Bake for 30 minutes. Can be served with vanilla ice cream.

GRANDMA'S FRUIT COBBLER

1 C. sifted flour	3 T. shortening
1 T. sugar	½ C. milk
1½ t. baking powder	½ C. sugar
½ t. salt	1 to 2 T. cornstarch
½ C. juice from fruit (add water to make ½ C. if necessary)	2 C. fruit (fresh peaches or plums are best)

Preheat oven to 400°. Sift flour, 1 tablespoon sugar, baking powder, and salt into a bowl. Cut in shortening, using two knives, until well blended. Stir in milk. Set aside.

Mix remaining sugar and cornstarch. Heat fruit juice, and add sugar mixture. Stir until thickened, then add fruit. Place in deep baking dish. Dot with butter and sprinkle with cinnamon. Drop dough by spoonfuls on top.

Bake 25-30 minutes or until golden brown. Serve warm.

HELEN'S FLYING SAUCER COOKIES

Sift together and set aside:

2½ C. flour	1½ t. baking soda
¾ t. baking powder	¾ t. salt

Cream together in a separate, larger bowl:

1⅓ C. margarine or butter	¾ C. brown sugar
2 C. sugar	

Add 2 eggs, the flour mixture, and 2 t. vanilla.
Then add:

2½ C. rolled oats	2½ C. coconut
2½ C. corn flakes	

Mix thoroughly.

Drop dough by large tablespoonfuls onto greased cookie sheet. Bake at 350°, 8-10 minutes. Do not overcook.

PARMESAN CHICKEN

2 C. grated Parmesan cheese
2 C. bread crumbs
½ lb. butter or margarine, melted

1 T. garlic salt
1 T. dry parsley flakes
6 chicken breasts cut in half

Mix all ingredients except butter and chicken. Dip chicken pieces in butter, then roll in and coat with crumb mixture. Place in baking dish side by side.

Bake 40 minutes at 350° or until cooked through and golden brown. Serve with Rice Pilaf (recipe follows).

RICE PILAF

Great side dish!
1 C. uncooked white rice
1 C. uncooked coil vermicelli (in pasta section)
¼ lb. butter
2½ C. boiling chicken broth

Brown vermicelli in butter (it must be broken into small pieces). Add rice and broth. Cover tightly, and do not stir until moisture is absorbed. Salt and pepper to taste.

SUNDAY POT ROAST

Wonderful to come home to after church on a winter day! Recipe can be doubled.

2 lb. pot roast of beef (or stew
    beef chunks)
4 medium potatoes
4 raw carrots, cut into chunks
4 stalks celery

1 large onion
1 green pepper
2 T. flour
salt & pepper
1 can cream of chicken soup

Put meat in bottom of heavy pot or baking dish; season with salt and pepper. Add vegetables. Sprinkle flour over all. Mix soup with ¼ cup water, and pour over top.

Cover tightly and bake 4-5 hours at 250° (or 3 hours at 325°).

ARTICHOKE APPETIZERS

We like this so much that we have it for breakfast Christmas morning.

2 6-oz. jars marinated artichoke hearts

⅛ t. each pepper, oregano, Tabasco sauce

1 small onion, finely chopped

1 clove garlic, minced

2 T. minced parsley

¼ t. salt

½ lb. sharp cheddar cheese, shredded

4 eggs

¼ C. fine dry bread crumbs

Drain marinade from one jar into frying pan. Drain other jar and discard marinade. Chop artichoke hearts, set aside. Add onion and garlic to frying pan; sauté till limp. Beat eggs, and mix in remaining ingredients. Then mix all ingredients together thoroughly. Pour into greased 7-by-11-inch pan. Bake at 325° for 30 minutes.

Let cool slightly, and cut into one- or two-inch squares. Delicious!

OMA'S HERB-FLAVORED POT ROAST

4-lb. round-bone roast

3 T. flour

1 t. salt

¼ t. pepper

3 T. shortening

1 beef bouillon cube

½ C. hot water

2 bay leaves

½ t. marjoram

½ t. each salt & pepper

½ t. parsley flakes

½ t. dried basil

Combine flour, 1 teaspoon salt, and ¼ teaspoon pepper. Sprinkle generously on each side of meat. Heat shortening in heavy pot, then brown the meat on each side. Pour off drippings. Dissolve bouillon cube in hot water. Add all herbs to bouillon. Pour over beef. Cook over low heat for 3-3 ½ hours. Remove bay leaves. Serve with gravy.

MOM'S POTATO SALAD

5 lbs. boiling potatoes

1 dozen eggs
8 stalks celery (tops included)
6-8 dill pickles
1-2 large onions

1 qt. mayonnaise (or less, depending on your preference)

1-2 T. mustard
a dash of pickle juice
salt & pepper to taste

Boil potatoes in jackets. Cool thoroughly. Peel and cut into bite-size pieces. Boil eggs 10-15 minutes; immediately immerse in ice-cold water. Peel and chop and add to potatoes. Chop and add celery, onion, and pickles. Add mayonnaise to your liking. Add mustard, pickle juice, salt, and pepper. Stir mixture thoroughly (we use our hands). Refrigerate thoroughly.

CREAM OF POTATO SOUP

3 C. onion, diced

2 ribs celery, chopped
1/4 lb. butter, melted
½ C. flour
1½ qts. chicken stock (broth)
salt and pepper

6 medium to large potatoes, diced

6 slices bacon, fried and drained

2 C. hot milk

Cook onions and celery in butter till tender. Add flour, blending well. Cook 3-4 minutes, but do not brown. Add half of the chicken broth, stirring until thickened and smooth. Remove from heat.

Cook potatoes in remaining chicken broth until done. Add to first mixture. Blend. Add hot milk. Add bacon and salt and pepper.

VEGETABLE SOUP

Simmer a large soup bone in 6 pints of water for half a day. Cool and refrigerate.

Next day, remove fat and bones and strain off scum.

Add the following and simmer:

1 T. salt	1 onion, chopped
1½ t. coarsely ground pepper	fresh basil
1 large can whole tomatoes, cut up (add juice as well)	
1 T. chopped parsley	1 green pepper, chopped

Two hours before serving, add:

2 potatoes, cubed	1 package frozen corn
several carrots, sliced	anything else you like

Serve with baking-powder biscuits.

RECIPES FOR THOSE WHO SAY, "I CAN'T MAKE PIE!"

FOOD PROCESSOR PIE CRUST

1 C. all-purpose flour	¼ C. plus 2 T. butter, frozen
1 t. salt	2-2½ T. ice water

Cut butter into six pieces. Combine flour, salt, and butter. Process until mixture looks like cornmeal. With processor running, add water a little at a time until ball forms. Cover and chill 30 minutes. Roll out and use as needed.

KATHY DODD'S OIL PIE CRUST

Mix in a pie pan:

1½ C. flour	½ t. salt
1 t. sugar	

Mix together ½ cup oil and 2 tablespoons milk, and stir into the above. Press around pan to form crust. (You don't even roll this one out!)

MIXER PASTRY

For 45 small tarts or 2 pies.

4 C. flour	1½ C. shortening
1½ t. salt	⅔ C. water

Set aside 1 cup flour out of the 1 pound. Mix the salt with the rest of the flour and cut in the shortening, using electric mixer. Mix the water into the reserved 1 cup flour, forming a paste. Add the paste to the flour and shortening, using the mixer to combine until it forms a ball. Divide and roll.

For 200 small tarts, follow above directions using these measurements:

6 lbs. flour (save 11/2 lbs. to mix into water for paste)	1½ oz. (3 T.) salt
4½ lbs. shortening (9 C.)	4 C. cold water

Or . . . keep a stock of ready-made pie crusts from the dairy case at your local supermarket!

MOM'S APPLE PIE

Heat oven to 425°. Prepare one of the previous pie crusts for a two-crust pie.

5-7 tart cooking apples, depending on size (Green Pippin are our favorite). Peel and slice apples thinly. Toss apples in large bowl with one cup of sugar mixed with one rounded teaspoon of cinnamon. Place apples in pastry-lined (unbaked) pie tin. Dot with butter. Place top crust over all, and flute the edges. Cut slits in top crust. Bake one hour till golden and apples are tender. Cool thoroughly.

Enjoy!

ANSWERS TO COMMON QUESTIONS

(Adapted from Two Ways to Live Trainee Workbook, Matthias Media, pages 45-49 [http://www.matthiasmedia.com.au])

Of the many questions that non-Christians pose as we share the gospel, some crop up again and again. Here is a sample of some of the most common questions, with some suggestions on how to answer.

1. *How do you know that God exists?*

Because he came to earth in Jesus.

We accept that Winston Churchill was Prime Minister of England during the Second World War because of the various historical records that exist. We mightn't have seen or heard him in person, but we trust the records. "Have you ever seen God?" "No, but I might have if I'd been born at the right time."

Jesus claimed to be God (see, for example, John 5:18; 20:28-29), and his actions bore out this claim. If you'd been there, you would have seen and heard him.

Read one of the Gospels for yourself, and check out his claims.

If he is God, then you should serve him as God.

(Further reading: *A Fresh Start* by John Chapman, Chaps. 6-8.)

2. *Can you trust the New Testament documents?*

Historical evidence in the New Testament is confirmed at a number of points by the non-Christian writers Tacitus and Josephus.

The New Testament documents are close in time to the figure of Jesus.

The documentation is extensive, coming from as many as ten authors, eight of whom wrote independently of each other.

The documents are historical in character as well as theological.

The text of these documents has come down to us intact from the era in which it was written.

(Further reading: *Is the New Testament History?* by Paul Barnett.)

3. Why does God allow suffering?

In the end we don't know why God allowed evil into the world.

Much suffering is a direct result of our own sinfulness (e.g., the suffering caused by drunkenness, or greed, or lust, or . . .).

But some is not (see John 9:1-3).

All suffering results from the fallen nature of our world (see Rom. 8:18-25).

God uses suffering to discipline and strengthen his children (Heb. 12:7-11; Rom. 5:3-5).

God does something about our suffering. Jesus suffered and died so that we could be forgiven and participate in the "new creation" where there will be no suffering.

(Further reading: *How to Give Away Your Faith* by Paul E. Little, Chap. 5.)

4. What happens to those who have never heard the gospel?

We can trust God to be just; he will judge people according to their response to what they know.

Everyone has received some revelation, even if only from the created order (see Rom. 1:18ff.).

Those who have more revealed to them will be held responsible (Matt. 11:20-24).

You have heard — so do something about it and leave the others to God.

(Further reading: *How to Give Away Your Faith* by Paul E. Little, Chap. 5.)

5. What about other religions?

Sincerity does not equal truth. One can be sincerely wrong.

If the different religions contradict each other (which they do at several major points), they cannot all be right.

The question really is: Has God revealed himself, and if so, how? Jesus claimed to be the unique revelation of God. He claimed to be God in the flesh. Are his claims valid? Investigate the New Testament. If he is God, the other religions are wrong.

The New Testament is clear that Jesus is the only way (Acts 4:12; John 14:6).

(Further reading: *So What's the Difference?* by Fritz Ridenour.)

6. Aren't all good people Christians?

What is "good"? How "good" is good enough?

Some of us are better than others, but no one meets God's standards (see Rom. 3:23).

God says that there is only one way, and it is not "being good" (John 14:6).

God is after friends, not "good" rebels. It's a matter of whose side you are on.

(Further reading: *A Fresh Start* by John Chapman, Chap. 11.)

7. Do you have to go to church to be a Christian?

This is similar in some ways to the "good people" question. God is not after churchgoers but friends.

You become God's friend by being forgiven and submitting to him, not by doing your duty at church.

Once you are in his family (by forgiveness), you will of course want to meet with other members of the family — one way to do this is to go to church. Church is God's family getting together.

8. Isn't faith only psychological?

If our faith is based purely on experience ("Christianity works for me"), then there is no way of arguing this objection. It might work for me because it's "true" because of my particular psychological upbringing or conditioning.

However, if Christianity is based on objective historical events (the death and resurrection of Jesus), the truth (or otherwise) of Christianity has nothing to do with our psychological state.

(Further reading: *How to Give Away Your Faith* by Paul E. Little, Chap. 5.)

9. Hasn't science disproved Christianity?

Most people mean, "Hasn't the theory of evolution replaced creation and so disproved Christianity?" (People usually aren't talking about archaeology, which, incidentally, backs up the Bible at almost every point.)

Avoid a technical discussion about evolution, carbon dating, etc. This gets nowhere.

Ask what conclusion they are drawing from the evolutionary stance: Did the world come into being by chance? Or did God make the world using certain evolutionary processes? The answer to that will reveal the person's presupposition about God's existence. *How* God made the universe is not as important a point as *that* he made it.

Steer the conversation toward talking about God's existence (see the first question above) and finally toward Jesus. If Jesus is God, that puts the creation/evolution debate in a new perspective. Emphasize that the person needs to find out if God exists before tackling creation/evolution, to read one of the Gospels, etc.

(Further reading: *Unnatural Enemies* by Kirsten Birkett.)

10. What about homosexuality?

An increasingly common question these days concerns Christian attitudes toward sexuality, and homosexuality in particular. *Aren't Christians just outdated bigots for opposing homosexuality?* An answer could go like this:

Do you think pedophilia is a natural and right way to behave?

(Assuming they say no) So it is at least a reasonable question to ask: Are some sexual practices wrong?

The question then becomes: How do we make a judgment about any particular sexual practice? By majority opinion? If that were so, then the earth was flat in the sixteenth century, Hitler was right in the late 1930s in Germany, and homosexuality was wrong about twenty years ago.

In the end, only the Creator has the right (and the wisdom) to declare something right or wrong. Only he has the authority, and only he has the complete picture.

If we accept who Jesus is, and therefore God's authority over the world, then we must listen to him — and he quite clearly says that homosexuality is not the way he created us to behave. It goes against the created order.

Even so, Christians don't hate homosexuals. We want to be kind and accepting of them, and help them to work through their struggles.

11. Aren't Christians hypocrites?

This question often relates to certain practices of Christians in history, such as the abuse of children by priests, alleged mistreatment of indigenous people by Christian missionaries, and so on.

Point out that Christians claim to be sinful. It is not hypocritical for us to err, for it is part of the fabric of our belief that we are rebels at heart and will continue to make mistakes. Christianity is about forgiveness, not perfect performance.

Also point out that Christians have done an almost incalculable amount of good in the world throughout history — that many of the things we take for granted (like health care, literacy, education, scientific endeavor, political freedom, the justice system, etc.) have all stemmed from Christianity and Christians. In fact, the good Christianity has done would far outweigh the bad. This does not make Christianity true, but it is rarely acknowledged.

Having said that, it is also not really fair to judge the truth of Jesus (who he was, what he did) by the bad behavior of some who claim to be his followers. Jesus himself indicated that in the future many people would claim to bear his name, but actually know nothing of him. When some of these people commit atrocities in his name, it is hardly Jesus' fault!

Nor does it have any bearing on whether you are going to accept Jesus' claim on your life. Those who do wrong will have to give account to God for their actions. And so will you.

NOTES

INTRODUCTION:
THINKING CHRISTIANLY ABOUT THE FAMILY

1. Robert L. Dabney, *Discussions: Evangelical and Theological*, Vol. 1 (London: Banner of Truth, 1967), 691.
2. C. S. Lewis, *The Four Loves* (London: Geoffrey Bles, 1960), 48.

DISCIPLINE OF
ESTABLISHING A HERITAGE

1. Robert Hughes, "The Fraying of America," *Time*, February 3, 1992, 45-46.
2. J. I. Packer, *Knowing God* (Downers Grove, IL: InterVarsity Press, 1973), 19-20.

DISCIPLINE OF
PROMOTING FAMILY AFFECTION

1. Phyllis McGinley, *The Province of the Heart* (New York: Dell, 1959), 72.
2. Elton Trueblood, *The Recovery of the Family* (New York: Harper and Brothers, 1953), 94.
3. Annie Dillard, *Teaching a Stone to Talk* (New York: Harper and Row, 1982), 187.
4. William Manchester, *The Last Lion*, Vol. 1 (Boston: Little, Brown, and Company, 1982), 36-37.

DISCIPLINE OF
CULTIVATING THE SOUL

1. Eleazar Mather, *A Serious Exhortation to the Present and Succeeding Generation in New England*, as quoted in Leland Ryken, *Worldly Saints: The Puritans as They Really Were* (Grand Rapids, MI: Zondervan, 1986), 83.
2. Benjamin Wadsworth, *The Well-Ordered Family*, as quoted in Ryken, *Worldly Saints: The Puritans as They Really Were*, 83.
3. Dorothy Walworth, "General of the Army: Evangeline Booth," *Reader's Digest*, 51, No. 304 (August 1947), 36-40.
4. Joseph T. Bayly, *Out of My Mind* (Grand Rapids, MI: Zondervan, 1993), 72-73.
5. Irwin Lutzer, radio interview on the Moody Bible Institute program *Nightline*.
6. Alister McGrath, "When Doubt Becomes Unbelief," *Tabletalk*, 16, No. 1 (January 1992), 8-10.

7. Cotton Mather, *Cares About the Nurseries*, as quoted in Ryken, *Worldly Saints: The Puritans as They Really Were*, 80.

DISCIPLINE OF
PRAYING WITH DEDICATION

1. Augustine, *Confessions*, 9.33.
2. H. G. Haile, *Luther: An Experiment in Biography* (Garden City, NY: Doubleday, 1980), 56.
3. Oswald Chambers, *Daily Thoughts for Disciples* (Fort Washington, PA: Christian Literature Crusade, 1976), 75.
4. E. M. Bounds, *Power Through Prayer* (Grand Rapids, MI: Zondervan, 1982), 28. Bounds quotes Edward Payson: "Prayer is the first thing, the second thing, the third thing necessary to minister. Pray, therefore, my dear brother, pray, pray, pray."

DISCIPLINE OF
INSTILLING HEALTHY SELF-REGARD

1. Jerry Adler, "Hey, I'm Terrific," *Newsweek*, February 17, 1992, 46.
2. Ibid., 51.
3. Ibid., 49, 51.
4. Paul Brownback, *The Danger of Self-Love* (Chicago: Moody Press, 1982), 51.
5. Henry Fairlie, *The Seven Deadly Sins Today* (South Bend, IN: University of Notre Dame, 1979), 31-32.
6. Paul Tournier, quoted by Don Matzat, *Christ Esteem* (Eugene, OR: Harvest House, 1990), 42.
7. Quoted by Don Matzat, *Christ Esteem*, 98.
8. Joanna McGrath and Alister McGrath, *The Dilemma of Self-Esteem* (Wheaton, IL: Crossway Books, 1992), 89-106.

USING APPROPRIATE DISCIPLINE

1. Robert Coles, "Discipline," *Family Weekly*, March 27, 1983, 4-5.
2. Cotton Mather, *Farewell Exhortation*, quoted by Leland Ryken, *Worldly Saints: The Puritans as They Really Were* (Grand Rapids, MI: Zondervan, 1986), 79.
3. Samuel Johnson, quoted by William Barclay, *The Letters to the Galatians and Ephesians* (Philadelphia: Westminster, 1958), 183.

DISCIPLINE OF
TEACHING GOOD MANNERS

1. James Howe, *The Muppet Guide to Magnificent Manners* (Toronto: Muppet Press/Random House, 1984), 22.
2. Edith Schaeffer, *Hidden Art* (Wheaton, IL: Tyndale, 1971), 123.

DISCIPLINE OF
FOSTERING LIFELONG ENRICHMENTS

1. Annie Dillard, *Pilgrim at Tinker Creek* (New York: Harper's Magazine Press, 1974), 129-130.
2. Geoffrey Norman, "A Fisherman's Seasons," in *The Ultimate Book of Fishing*, eds. Lee Eisenberg and DeCourcy Taylor (Boston: Houghton Mifflin, 1981), 20.

APPENDIX:
ADVENT TREE INSTRUCTIONS

1. Thanks to the following for their work on this project: Kathleen and Niel Nielson — project coordination/editing; Gail and Richard Johnson — craft projects/art.

APPENDIX:
MAKING A PRAYER NOTEBOOK

1. Gerard Manley Hopkins, from St. Francis Xavier, "O Deus Ego Amo Te," in *A Treasury of Poems for Worship and Devotion*, ed. Charles L. Wallis (New York: Harper and Brothers, 1959), 98-99.

Scripture Index

GENERAL INDEX